D0377810

CATCH
THE
AGE WAVE

259.3
A742c

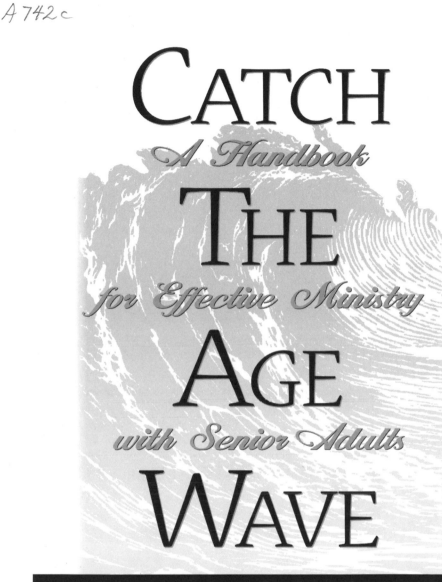

CATCH

A Handbook

THE

for Effective Ministry

AGE

with Senior Adults

WAVE

Win Arn and Charles Arn

Beacon Hill Press of Kansas City
Kansas City, Missouri

Copyright 1999
by Beacon Hill Press of Kansas City

ISBN 083-411-8009

Printed in the
United States of America

Cover Design: Mike Walsh

Scripture quotations not otherwise identified are from the *Holy Bible, New International Version*® (NIV®). Copyright © 1973, 1978, 1984 by International Bible Society. Used by permission of Zondervan Publishing House. All rights reserved.

Permission to quote from the following copyrighted sources is acknowledged with appreciation:

The *New Testament in Modern English* (PHILLIPS), Revised Student Edition, by J. B. Phillips, translator. Copyright 1958, 1960, 1972 by J. B. Phillips.

The *Revised Standard Version* (RSV) of the Bible, copyright 1946, 1952, 1971 by the Division of Christian Education of the National Council of the Churches of Christ in the USA.

The *Living Bible* (TLB), © 1971. Used by permission of Tyndale House Publishers, Inc., Wheaton, IL 60189.

The King James Version (KJV).

Library of Congress Cataloging-in-Publication Data

Arn, Win.
   Catch the age wave : a handbook for effective ministry with senior adults / Win Arn and Charles Arn.
      p.   cm.
   Originally published: Grand Rapids, MI : Baker Books, c1993.
   Includes bibliographical references.
   ISBN 0-8341-1800-9
   1. Church work with the aged Handbooks, manuals, etc.   I. Arn, Charles.   II. Title.
[BV4435.A76   1999]
259'.3—dc21   99-24414
                                                                              CIP

10   9   8   7   6   5   4   3   2   1

Contents

Introduction

～ ～ ～

There is a tide in the affairs of men,
Which, taken at the flood, leads on to fortune;
Omitted, all the voyage of their life
Is bound in shallows and in miseries.[1]

Who can deny that the "age wave," just starting to break on our national shores, provides a flood-tide opportunity for the church? But just to know about this demographic phenomenon is no guarantee that a church will catch the wave. In fact, the possibility of most churches doing so is fairly remote, given the present set of attitudes, activities, and priorities.

It is to this condition that *Catch the Age Wave: A Handbook for Effective Ministry with Senior Adults* addresses itself. Not only does this volume seek to blow the bugle—to arouse the church to its great opportunity—but it supplies the principles and methodology to accomplish the task. The "graying" of America, we believe, could spark the *growing* of the church, if adult ministries are given greater priority. Of the approximately 250 million persons who now live in the United States, half are over age 45. And the average age of Americans will continue to rise in the future.

Of these "older adults" who are church members, 66 percent are members of what are often called mainline churches (Presbyterian, Methodist, Lutheran, Episcopal, Church of Christ, etc.). With birthrates in these denominations averaging half of a child below their annual membership replacement figures,[2] the obvious conclusion is that many of these churches could disappear in the next generation. This is especially tragic in light of the fact that in proximity to most of these churches are large numbers of senior adults who are bereft of the knowledge of Jesus Christ and the caring community of a local congregation.

For church leaders who place a priority on communicating the gospel to men and women who are presently outside the church, this book will be of great value. We believe that the Great Commission—to "go and make disciples"—is a primary responsibility of the church, a responsibility that surely extends to the senior adult group. Christians at every age are called to have a part in God's mission of reconciliation by reaching out to those outside the community of faith.

The age wave is coming. Will you and your church be ready for it?

Although the book is a joint effort, the first-person pronouns refer to Win Arn.

PART ONE

~ ~ ~

Understanding Age-Wave Issues in Relation to the Church

~ ~ ~

1

The Church of Tomorrow

There is no longer doubt among social scientists and political observers that the American culture is experiencing cataclysmic changes. *Time* magazine observed that the change of the millennium has "become a transforming boundary between one age and another, between a scheme of things that is disintegrating and another that is taking shape."[1]

The changes are affecting everyone from the farmer in Nebraska to the single mother in Los Angeles. The pace of these changes will accelerate. Even now, America is rapidly aging! Social scientists are convinced that this population shift—the "graying" of its citizens—will soon produce the most profound social revolution in our history. "It's going to be of a significance that matches the dawn of the industrial age or the invention of the microchip," says Ken Dychtwald, noted social scientist and demographic observer.[2]

Even now, every institution in society is being forced to understand and adapt to dramatic age-related changes. Entire nations are experiencing breathtaking transformations as traditions give way to new ideas. Medical discoveries and technological advances are daily occurrences, and communication is changing the way we think about and understand our world. The words from the film *Fiddler on the Roof,* "It's a new world, Gulda!" are even more true today.

As American society moves from one age to the next, the church, too, is experiencing changes. For those of us concerned with seeing the local church function as a relevant and vital part of Americans' lives in the future, today's cultural trends are important to understand.[3]

There is a widening contrast between churches that are perceived by Americans as presenting relevant answers to the issues and challenges of the day, and churches seen as old, outdated, and irrelevant. This will increasingly mark a distinction between vitality and relevance for some churches—and stagnation and obsolescence for others. The distinctions cross denominational boundaries, theological persuasions, geographical regions, pastoral styles, and church size. The dichotomy between relevant and irrelevant churches is becoming visible in this changing of the millennium and will become even more evident in the next decade. In its simplest form, some churches will have contextualized their message to the society around them; others will have retained outdated methods and lost their audience.

What will characterize these "effective" churches of tomorrow? How will they be distinctive? The answer is: *Their paradigms will have changed.* A "paradigm" is defined as "a grid of values and rules through which life is interpreted and understood." Paradigms provide structures for solving problems and strategies for accomplishing goals. Paradigms are why people—and churches—do things and how they believe things should be done. They are the lenses through which the world is seen and interpreted.

Effective churches will confront the issues of their changing society while retaining their basic theological truths. They will change their ministry paradigms to reflect their changing context. They will have found that many of their old paradigms no longer allow them to accomplish effective ministry and outreach.

Below is a list of paradigms under which many churches operated in the mid-1900s but that became outdated by the turn of the century. Across from the old is a new paradigm that has emerged or is emerging.

OLD PARADIGMS	NEW PARADIGMS
### *Senior Adults*	
Require volunteers	Source of volunteers
Caretakers	Caregivers
Apathetic outreach to seniors	Intentional outreach to seniors
"Traditional senior" attitudes and stereotypes	"New senior" attitudes (see chapter 2)
One senior adult group and program	Multiple senior adult groups and programs
Retirement motive: play	Retirement motive: work, learn, serve, play
### *Volunteers*	
Sacrifice self	Maximize self
Members serve institution	Institution serves members
Volunteers	Paid employees
### *Evangelism*	
Confrontational	Relational
Mass approach	Personal approach
Targets general population	Targets specific people groups
Single presentation	Multiple exposure
Single method	Multiple methods
Goal: a decision	Goal: a disciple
America: a Christian nation	America: a secularized mission field
Goal: church membership	Goal: Christian discipleship
Motive: guilt	Motive: value and love
### *Pastor and Staff*	
Enabler	Initiator
Activity-oriented	Achievement-oriented
Teaching style: propositional	Teaching style: experiential
Selection based on credentials and denominational history	Selection based on performance
Church staff drawn from seminary	Church staff drawn from congregation

Christian Education

Sunday evening service	Family nights
Sunday School	Small groups
Age groupings	Lifestyle groupings
One weekly meeting time and place	Numerous meeting times and places
Verbal-oriented	Visual-oriented

Facilities

Sanctuary	Multipurpose room
Considered adequate	Regularly upgraded

Worship

Presentation	Participation
Intellectual	Experiential
Focus on Christians	Focus also on non-Christians

Examining your own church's paradigms in each of these categories is a helpful exercise for preparing your church for the 21st century. Even more important, however, is your church's willingness to evaluate its ministry paradigms honestly and its willingness to change those paradigms if necessary. The answer to these questions will also show whether your church is moving toward a future of growth and new outreach or is perpetuating traditions that will cause it to be seen as increasingly obsolete by unchurched persons in your community.

The scope of this book is focused on the first category of the ministry paradigms listed: senior adults. This is a particularly important area for church leaders to be concerned with—because (as you will discover in the next chapter) our society is being engulfed by a gigantic "age wave." The increasing number of older adults in our nation will become a larger and larger factor for effective church ministry and growth for the duration of our lifetimes. How could a church desirous of effective ministry fail to recognize that one of four people in society is a senior adult? Old paradigms for a senior adult ministry are even now inadequate and will become more so. New paradigms for the new senior are required.

CHURCHES THAT REACH NEW SENIORS

The new senior is so different from what most church leaders have grown up thinking older adults to be that an old approach to this new group will be as fruitless as fishing with a net full of holes. Here are some characteristics of the church that will successfully minister to and reach the new senior:

1. *Concerns of middle and older age will dominate the agenda of the church.* What are these concerns? Certain characteristics and themes mark these new seniors. One is the desire to be *comfortable.* Having worked and been responsible for earning a living for themselves and often for a family for most of their lives, they are inclined toward stress-free activities and situations. The church sanctuary and its environment—including the educational classrooms, the church's expectations, and the benefits of membership—will need to accommodate the comfort needs and expectations of the new senior.

Leisure activities with a purpose will become increasingly important for the church that desires to reach the new seniors. Travel trips will be goal-oriented. Vacation homes and RVs will assume new prominence in the lives of these church members. This leisure mentality offers the creative, aggressive church many opportunities to wed such interests and priorities with the overall purpose and direction of the church.

Health and wellness will be a concern of more and more people, and the church will need to address this. In middle and older age, maintenance of health is a crucial issue. Health-related material already abounds in magazines and newsletters, a trend that will increase. A few churches, recognizing this trend, have added a registered nurse to their staff. Similarly, nutrition and exercise will be of growing interest to senior adults. Exercise classes, bicycle clubs, and walking fellowships are already being seen in many churches. The church gym/family center (if there is one) will move from being dominated by youth to being shared with adults. Sports programs compatible with the energy, interests, and abilities of older adults will be offered. Church suppers and the tradition-bound potluck will become more ori-

ented to healthful consumption, and coffee breaks will be up-
graded with carrots, celery sticks, and fresh fruit.

The most nutritious meals in town may be those served at
the church—low in sodium, low in fat, low in sugar. Such foods
will become standard as courses on nutrition are added and
members become increasingly savvy about nutritional needs.
The church that builds wellness into its ministry will have an
edge in appealing to the flood of baby boomers who are moving
into middle and older age.

2. *The effective church of tomorrow will provide opportunities for using retirement years meaningfully.* Freed from the
pressures and demands of work and parenting, retirement for
the Christian new seniors will be a time for using their experiences and skills in service to Christ. Churches that do not present such a challenge and opportunity will lose lay membership
skills and training that could be significantly used in their mission. Perry and Peggy Hendricks typify the new seniors' concern for "meaning" in their retirement years:

> The rooster signaled another dawn. Joining the preco-
> cious bird came the cacophony of barking dogs, bicycle
> bells, and the friendly banter of street vendors. A child's cry
> drifted through the open window. Instinctively, Peggy moved
> to comfort her grandbaby, only to remember that child slept
> thousands of miles away. The wail that pierced her sleep fog
> belonged to another child in the already crowded street be-
> low. After a quick porridge breakfast, the couple would join
> those on the teeming streets dodging rickshaws and bicycles,
> bargaining for the day's food, stopping to chat with the beg-
> gars they knew by name, avoiding the open sewage, yet smil-
> ing at the women drawing water too near it. Soon Perry
> would be deep in paperwork, and Peggy would be tutoring
> English to a young Nepali man before starting in her office.
> Ah, they smiled, this is retirement![4]

The church and/or denomination that desires to minister
effectively to the new senior will provide opportunities for retirement-age seniors to minister to others. In so doing, they will

advance the cause of Christ and His Church in the world and bring joy, purpose, and fulfillment to those participating.

3. *Volunteerism will be different in the church of tomorrow.* New senior adults prize time very highly. Because it is their most precious asset, they will do all within their power to allocate it wisely and on their own terms. In a focus group with senior adults,[5] one of the members began listing the various jobs he was doing in the church. As he explained it, the worst part was that these regular commitments kept him from doing some traveling and enjoying the leisure of his retirement. He said that he was far more willing to come to the church and paint a wall (at least he knew when the job was finished) than to take a responsibility that went on and on and on.

Meaningful volunteerism among older adults is widespread: "Every day in the United States, seniors contribute 163,000 hours of volunteer work."[6] At minimum wage, that would amount to over $800,000 per day, or $200,000,000 per year. "Volunteerism" appears on the cover of national newsmagazines, gets into politics as "a thousand points of light," and is regularly profiled in TV documentaries.

While there will always be volunteers serving the church, the nature of their activities will change. Short-term responsibilities will replace long-term roles. One-time tasks will replace ongoing projects. Meaningful work will replace busywork. The church throughout its history has relied heavily on volunteers and will need to do so in the future. Most older volunteers are working for religious groups. This group of seniors represents 66 percent of all volunteer hours.[7]

For centuries, churches and denominations have been powered by volunteerism—be it serving on various boards and councils, chairing special projects, or teaching Sunday School. The volunteers of tomorrow will be no less committed, but they will have a different agenda than in the past.

4. *In the church of tomorrow, ministries of love and caring—both giving and receiving—will receive a high priority.* "Intimate relationships make a profound difference in the qual-

ity of life at any age," says Ken Dychtwald in *Age Wave.* "Yet, in later years of life, the making and keeping of relationships can become more difficult."[8]

The church of tomorrow will be helping members focus outside their own problems and concerns by learning about and practicing agape love. Love is a great lifesaver for senior adults who experience it. Without love, all else seems incomplete, purposeless, empty of any meaning.

Based on a research study we conducted several years ago and recently reevaluated in light of the age variable, older adults seem to be the group most able to give and receive love. For example, among those who participate in church Bible classes, 94 percent of adults over the age of 65 indicated they experience a high degree of love and caring in their classes. By contrast, only 65 percent of young adults (age 21-49) reported that same intensity of love and caring in class. Among adults between the ages of 51 and 65, 78 percent expressed feeling such emotions in their classes.

Respondents were asked: "On a scale of 1 to 10 [with 10 as "easiest"], how easy is it to say 'I love you' to the following persons?" Figure 1 shows the results in graph form.

Apparently it becomes easier for us to say "I love you" the older we become. With only a few exceptions, there is an increase at every age level, in every category. It is interesting to note that it appears easier for people over 65 years to say "I love you" to their friends (at the bottom of their list) than it is for young people under age 20 to say those same words to their own family members. The church of tomorrow will recognize the need for and attraction to love and will build it into their agendas.

5. *The development of spiritual maturity will be assigned greater priority.* The new senior realizes that there is a progression to life and that moving to the next step is a developmental challenge at all stages of the life cycle. Older adults who are longtime Christians, as well as those who are new believers, will need to feel a sense of progress in their spiritual lives. They will have little interest in investing time in areas of church life that

Figure 1.
Age Variables in Ease of Saying "I Love You"

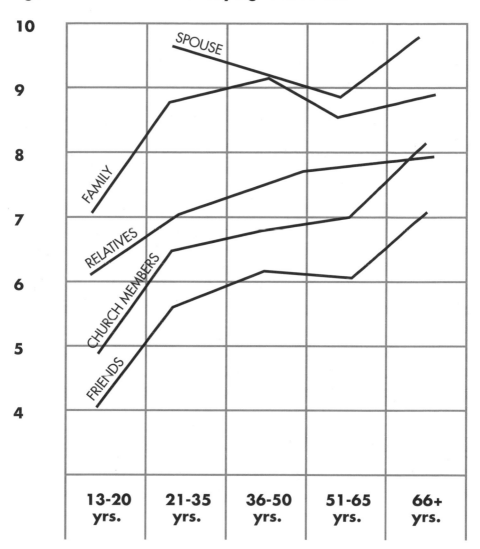

are nonproductive in terms of personal/spiritual benefit. Instead, they will want to make a contribution with their remaining time and talent.

My friend and personal mentor—new senior Dr. Donald McGavran—at 92 years said, "Some people think their lives stop when they retire, that their real work has ended. When I retired at age 68, the most important work of my life began. I strongly believe that real life is only beginning at retirement, and probably the most important contribution will be made by individuals during those years. But we must deal with important matters: matters of the church, matters of bringing people to Christ." Dr. McGavran was emphasizing a concern with enlarging one's inner life, the life of the spirit, and then having that inner life work itself out in meaningful service.

The church of tomorrow will see aging not as a descending process but as an ascending journey toward new horizons soon to be opened. Such a view does not yearn for what used to be. Rather, it seeks to find ways of harvesting all the experiences of a lifetime so that the senior years bring forth a heightened sense of contribution and worth. This desire for deeper meaning in life usually begins somewhere between 35 and 45 years of age—often called the midlife crisis. When individuals begin to define themselves in new ways, the drive for profit, pride, position, and power begins to yield slowly to purpose: "Why am I here? What am I meant to do?"

Bible studies that deal with issues faced by senior adults will take on new importance. A church that has a strong Bible teaching ministry will be well attended by this age-group, particularly as the baby boomers (those born between 1946 and 1964) join their ranks.

Susan H. McFadden, of the University of Wisconsin at Oshkosh, presented a paper to the Gerontological Society of America in which she said, "We need to learn more about the role of emotion in spirituality; and in particular, we need to listen carefully to the witness of great numbers of older people who may be serving as a kind of spiritual vanguard leading us all into a new century."

6. *The church of tomorrow will give more priority to adult ministry.* The demographics demand this! Over 76 percent of the total United States population is now composed of adults. Note especially the trends and projection related to the older adult population in figure 2.

FIGURE 2. POPULATION, BY AGE: 1960—2080

(Numbers in thousands.) Includes Armed Forces overseas.

Year	Total	Age (years)										
		Under 5	5-13	14-17	18-24	25-34	35-44	45-64	65 and over	85 and over	100 and over
Estimates											
1960	180,671	20,341	32,965	11,219	16,128	22,919	24,221	36,203	16,675	940	3
1965	194,303	19,824	35,754	14,153	20,293	22,465	24,447	38,916	18,451	1,082	(NA)
1970	205,052	17,166	36,672	15,924	24,712	25,323	23,150	41,999	20,107	1,430	5
1975	215,973	16,121	33,919	17,128	28,005	31,471	22,831	43,801	22,696	1,821	(NA)
1980	227,757	16,458	31,095	16,142	30,350	37,626	25,868	44,515	25,704	2,269	15
1985	239,279	18,004	30,110	14,865	28,749	42,238	31,839	44,934	28,540	2,695	28
1990	251,897	18,944	32,528	13,292	26,352	44,186	37,976	46,955	31,665	3,274	58
1995	265,151	19,497	34,686	14,651	24,704	41,716	42,624	52,989	34,286	4,035	87
2000	278,228	19,429	36,085	15,593	25,870	38,409	44,593	62,168	36,081	4,945	132
Projections											
2005	294,710	19,995	36,368	16,551	27,809	37,645	42,176	72,795	38,370	5,963	200
2010	305,882	21,194	36,925	16,654	29,212	39,546	38,934	80,890	42,527	7,160	294
2020	335,022	23,307	40,971	17,376	29,811	43,627	40,033	81,891	58,007	8,588	544
2030	362,327	24,285	43,978	19,448	32,633	44,698	44,070	77,763	75,452	11,256	867
2040	388,123	26,124	46,205	20,409	35,474	49,047	45,151	83,124	82,589	17,856	1,212
2050	413,580	27,664	49,624	21,669	37,015	52,550	49,405	88,207	87,445	24,117	2,286
2080	501,483	32,431	58,208	25,647	43,892	61,520	58,858	107,034	113,892	33,908	5,919

NA Not available.

Source: Current Population Reports. Senes P-25. Nos. 519.917.1022: Jacob S. Siegel and Jeffrey S. Passel. "New Estimates of the Number of Centenahans in the United States." *Journal of the American Statistical Association.* Vol. 71. No. 355.

Although it is helpful to think of various developmental stages for adults, "lifestyle" classifications are more descriptive, because there can be variations within age-groups. However, as a general classification, the following categories will suffice:

Young adults	21 to 49 years of age
Middle adults	50 to 64 years of age
Senior adults	65 to 79 years of age
Elderly	80+ years of age

While there will continue to be effective ministries for children and youth in most churches, the spiritual needs of adults will come into clearer focus. This includes those over 65, especially the new senior, a different breed from what the church has seen before.

7. *The church of tomorrow will provide leadership and structure for an effective senior adult ministry.* Let's consider leadership first. What are the specific qualities that a leader should possess to reach and nurture this group? The most important quality—and without which failure is certain—is a genuine love and concern for older adults. With love you cannot fail, and without it you cannot succeed.

In addition to this overriding compassion, a leader of senior adults needs to *like* older people. The leader will enjoy being in their company, sharing ideas, stories, conversation, and planning activities with them. Otherwise, a leader will be ineffective in his or her ministry.

A third requirement is a willingness to share leadership responsibility. While a leader might be officially appointed to head a group of seniors, it must be *their* program. The leader might help facilitate and coordinate activities, but the senior adults will respond positively only if they have ownership of the agenda.

Another quality for leadership of senior adults is a willingness to learn. Any formal training in gerontology that the leader may have acquired is all to the good, but informal education is also valuable. A leader should read widely in the field and subscribe to magazines and newsletters for seniors.

In any worthy venture, a successful leader will have a vision of what can and should be accomplished. This vision, with God's help and an abundance of faith and work, will accomplish miracles. We can certainly apply Scripture to senior adult ministry: "Where there is no vision, the people perish" (Prov. 29:18, KJV).

What age should a leader of senior adults be? As actress Billie Burke said, "Age doesn't matter unless you are cheese." Many seniors can qualify as leaders and thereby establish a new career, but some youth directors are being retrained for dual ministry to both youth and seniors. Although a Christian education director may be a natural for this role, some retirees see this leadership opportunity as a way to maximize their own life and ministry. Don't worry about age. Worry about being loving enough.

Concerning structure, it seems advisable to have representatives of the group serve on the official board of the church. This recognition gives importance to the ministry to senior adults, as well as providing a voice for them in church decisions and priorities. The senior ministry should be in the mainstream of the church's life and flow, not in some backwater.

Share your vision with your pastor. Keep channels of communication open. If the pastor understands and identifies with the group, he or she will want to further this ministry. Don't be surprised if the pastor suggests that the church have a Senior Sunday, when older adults are recognized for their achievements—past, present, and future—and challenged toward even higher Christian commitment.

2
The Senior Surge

O urs is an age of extended longevity. During most of human history, only 1 in 10 people lived to age 65. Today 8 in 10 zoom past that birthday. Older adults have become the fastest-growing segment of the population in the United States, their numbers outpacing teenagers for the first time ever. This group has created an age wave—a senior surge that is transforming the national landscape in many ways.

SOME MIND-BOGGLING STATISTICS

Two-thirds of all persons 65 or older who have ever lived are alive today.[1] American seniors now outnumber the entire population of Canada. Ten years have been added to the median age of the U.S. population since 1900.[2] Since 1950, the number of Americans over 100 years old has grown more than 10 times. By 2080, the centenarian population is expected to increase by a factor of 75.[3] In 1900, adults over 65 represented 4 percent of the population. The numbers have now jumped to nearly 14 percent. Demographers project that adults in that age-group will comprise 17.3 percent of the population in 2020.

By 2040, when the last of the baby boomers reach retirement age, 25 percent of the American population will be over 65. This will represent 87 million adults, or the equivalent of 174 new cities of 300,000 people each.

This phenomenon is not limited to the United States. In fact, the U.S. Census Bureau's international data base lists the United States as only 18th among longevous nations. As of the year 2000, senior adults worldwide number approximately 600,000,000.[4] Using the previous analogy, these 600,000,000 people translate into 1,200 cities, each with a population of 500,000. Here's another way to visualize the number of seniors in the world—if these 600,000,000 people were to hold hands and stretch their arms, the line would go to the moon, back to earth, and to the moon again. Or the line would cross the continental United States 227 times.

This worldwide "age wave," as Ken Dychtwald terms it,[5] has been duly noted by business and industry. Of every dollar spent for consumer goods in the United States, 40 cents is spent by persons over 50. This group of Americans presents a ripe opportunity for the church, since the population is projected to double in size over the next four decades.[6] But business as well as religious leaders are beginning to learn that older adults are not easily typecast. Effective communication strategies to attract this group are not just a matter of simply changing a few words or images.

One organization that is finding effective ways to communicate to older adults is A.A.R.P (American Association of Retired Persons). Its magazine, *Modern Maturity,* has a circulation of 22,430,894, far surpassing every other publication, including *Reader's Digest, TV Guide,* and *National Geographic.* This organization has a membership estimated to grow at a rate of approximately 8,000 new members a day.

Looking across the American church, one can note an absence of effective congregational ministries that focus on the life experiences and spiritual needs of persons over 55. There are also few opportunities that challenge individuals to devote a significant portion of their retirement years in service to others through the church. The church needs to awaken to the needs and potential that this senior surge represents.

DEFINING THE NEW SENIOR

The A.A.R.P. defines "seniors" as people over 50. The Social Security Administration uses the more arbitrary figure of 65 years. What can we call them? Marketing research indicates they do not like to be called "elderly," "senior citizens," or "golden-agers." Some have tried "whoopies" (short for well-heeled older people). Others refer to "opals" (older persons with active lifestyles) or "grumpies" (grown-up, mature people). The latest term being used is "the chronologically gifted." But none of these labels have taken hold. Perhaps "senior" does not represent a numerical age or a designated lifestyle. It has to do more with atti tudes—how people see *themselves!* What exactly is a *new* senior?

Identifying new seniors is not difficult. Although this has little to do with age alone, they are often the soon-to-be-retired or recently retired. Yet, they can be 75, 85, or 90+ years old.

Basically, new seniors are distinguished from their peers in their outlook on life and the way this outlook is implemented in their activities, attitudes, and approach to life. *U.S. News and World Report* says about this growing segment of the population: "What is important about this new generation is its difference not only in size, but in vitality and outlook."[7]

We see seniors in television programming and in Hollywood films. We notice them leaving with an RV caravan that is heading for Mexico to help build a church, serving as hospital volunteers, sitting in college classrooms, or striding across a golf course. We will not, however, see them lounging at home in a rocking chair, bored and lonely. Instead, we look for them on the bike path.

New seniors do not think of themselves as old or declining. (They would rarely attend a senior citizens group.) They view the future as a time of harvest and renewal rather than the beginning of a cold winter. These people function on new assumptions about living. If retired, they see the gift of new free time as an opportunity for work, for learning, for service, for growing, and for play. They are focused on the present and the future, not on the past; on serving, not on being served; on involvement, not on disengagement.

New seniors who are Christians recognize this stage of life as an opportunity to serve Christ and His Church, a chance to make a contribution through their experience, their skills, their knowledge, their energy, and the other resources they have developed. Fulfilling these dreams is a motivating challenge.

New seniors have goals and objectives superimposed on their memories and history. They intend to keep growing and discovering and to join with others of similar mind-set and lifestyle. These people hold the key to a changed view of aging for the church and the entire nation. The church that provides opportunities for older adults to fulfill their dreams and goals will be the church able to reach this rapidly growing generation of Americans.

DEBUNKING STEREOTYPES

Some cartoonists would have you think that all senior adults are alike. Older men are often depicted as disheveled hunchbacks with a bulbous jaw, missing teeth, and a wooden cane to help them take short, faltering steps. Older women are often drawn as "bag ladies" with straggly, unkempt hair, wrinkled clothes, and a failing memory.

The truth is that Americans over 55 cannot be characterized so simplistically. Looking below the surface, one discovers an amazing variety. Some older adults are wonderfully sweet and flexible; others have become sour and brittle. Some have a great vision for tomorrow; others refuse to live for today and retreat into the past. Some enjoy robust health and vitality; others suffer many physical infirmities. Some are materially wealthy; others are pathetically poor. Some are spiritually enriched with a vital faith; others are devoid of any hope for eternity. Older adults are as different and changing as the reflections in a kaleidoscope.

More specifically, the spiritual maturity of older adults varies greatly. An adult of 70 who started attending church at the age of 10 could have been exposed to as many as 6,000 sermons, not to mention special church events, Sunday School classes, and various devotionals. Such experiences have often contributed toward making "saints" of these men and women. In other cases, the same spiritual exposure seems to have been dissipated, like water off a duck's back. Many older adults, even those presently unchurched, have had varying exposure to church or spiritual teaching. Others have no religious memory and have become increasingly secularized, as has the nation and the rest of the world. A great challenge for the church is to develop programs, activities, and concepts that will develop spirituality among its adult population (see chapter 10).

One observer writes, "It is estimated that 25% 35% of the members of most major faith groups are over 65 years old, whereas seniors compose just 12% of the general population."[8] While the figure varies considerably from one denomination or church to another, more senior adults are members of churches than are members of nearly any other organization.

GENERATIONAL DIFFERENCES

Sociologists and astute religious observers have noted that people born prior to World War II have a different set of values from those born after that time. Sociologists call this the cohort effect, and it is a useful way to understand the values and preferences of various generations. Compare older adults and baby boomers in the chart on the next page.

From these observations, we can identify a set of values common to many older adults and clearly see implications for reaching this group. People over 55 tend to:

1. Respond to teaching.
2. Be willing to sacrifice personally for a worthy goal or cause.
3. Prefer stability.
4. Resist rapid change.

PERSONS BORN BEFORE 1939
(Older Adults)

Respond well to teaching

Sacrifice of self

Focus on group goals

Communal ethics

Serve the institution

Pursuit of "success"—career, family, and institutional goals

Leadership by command, directives, position

Standardization valued

Resistance to change

Common religious heritage

Hierarchical structures

Financially: "Save, save"

PERSONS BORN BETWEEN 1946 AND 1964
(Baby Boomers)

Respond well to interaction

Maximization of self

Focus on individual goals

Individualized ethics

Served by the institution

Pursuit of "success"—career and goals modified by inner fulfillment

Leadership by influence, ideas, relationships

Innovation valued

Insistence on change

Minimal religious heritage

Horizontal structures

Financially: "Spend, spend"

5. Prefer to associate with those of like beliefs/values.
6. Respect authority.
7. Believe in the value of institutions and are willing to serve to ensure their success/survival.
8. Have a high degree "loyalty" (marriage, brands, church, employer, institutions, clubs).
9. Consider volunteering as both a privilege and a responsibility.

Implications for Church Programming for Seniors

Based on the values outlined above, educational designers have found that certain learning techniques are more successful with older adults than with other groups. For a church, these teaching strategies would include the following principles:

1. *Providing opportunities for meaningful service.* Don't try to simply educate or entertain. Examples of this are mission trips, community service projects, convalescent ministry, senior choirs.

2. *Making sure the church's goals are compatible with the general values of older adults.* In other words, the activities should have a recognizable worth or benefit that is clearly communicated to the participants. Although strategy may be specified (and explained), the program must be "owned" by those who will implement it.

3. *Before instituting change, ensuring the potential for success.* This means clearly establishing and explaining the need for change; providing an opportunity for ongoing input, feedback, and revision; and obtaining consensus on the nature and rate of change.

4. *Targeting the ministry to those seniors your church can best reach.* However, although serving seniors already in the congregation is a mutually beneficial endeavor, planning might include a future outreach to other older adults in the community.

5. *Developing activities that both build and reward loyalty to the church and the program itself.* This is achieved by establishing within each individual a sense of personal accomplishment through identification with a like-minded group of people with similar goals.

WHAT ABOUT THE FUTURE?

The shape of tomorrow can already be seen on the horizon. In almost every field, the age wave is beginning to make a significant impact. In politics, lawmakers are increasingly tuning in to the voices of older adults, and their influence is being felt at the ballot box. In travel, those 55 years and older account for over 80 percent of all leisure-travel dollars, and the number is growing. In medicine, the search is intensifying for answers to the symptoms of aging.

Changes in lifestyles of older adults are also impacting the morals and cultural standards of our society. In entertainment, there are more and more older adult models used in programming and advertising. In education, older adults are going to college in record numbers, and some educators foresee that soon the majority of college students will be adults over 50. In sports, traditional age limitations are being stretched farther and farther. In the printed media, there has been astounding increase in the number of people 55 and older who are featured in books and magazine articles. Rhea Rubin found that, in the early '80s, it was difficult to find realistic portrayals of older people in novels, stories, poems, and plays. Today, there are many novels and short stories portraying older people—all of which have come into existence in the years since.[9]

But what about the church? Today, in the average congregation, one-third to one-half are over 55. In coming years, as pastors look over their Sunday morning worship service, they will notice that a majority of their attenders have white hair. The church's fixation on youth will be modified, and older adults will be targeted as a receptive and desired audience. Many more staff persons will need to be employed to focus on programming for this group. Much will be learned about unique approaches to an outreach to older adults as more studies are conducted and more experience gained.

Some churches will far outdistance others in effective ministry to seniors in the population, because their leaders prepared early for the impact of the age wave. These churches will be modeling ministries of such life-changing proportions that older adults will be driving and leading the rest of the church. In contrast, churches without vital senior adult programs will be looked upon as being out of step with the times, missing out on a great opportunity for service and impact.

How to Catch the Age Wave

Let's look at the art of wave catching. Most people are attracted to the ocean, with its energy and power, its ever-changing waves. At most beaches there are surfers with their boards, watching and waiting for "the big one." These surfers can help illustrate where the church is in relation to the age wave—and also where it *should* be.

Some would-be surfers never go near the water. Although they dress properly and have their boards at hand, they just sit on the beach, talking among themselves and watching the waves break on the sand. They are not at the beach to swim but to get a tan, show off their fancy suits and boards, and talk about the big waves they have caught in the past. Sad to say, many churches, too, are "sitting on the beach," not really wanting to get wet—they just want to show off their beautiful buildings and discuss the good old days.

Another group of surfers can be seen paddling slowly out to where the action is, as if they want to be part of what's happening. When they see a wave cresting, they hurry to turn their boards in the right direction, but their timing is off. Before they know it, the swell has gone under them and headed for the shore, leaving them in the backwash. Some churches are like that—so slow to recognize an oncoming wave that by the time it arrives, they are too late to do anything but watch it go by.

Still other surfers are out where the big waves roll, sitting on their boards, eagerly watching. When they see a big one coming, they flop down on their boards and start paddling faster and faster, until the energy of the wave catches them, and they jump to their feet for the ride of their lives.

There are a few churches and pastors with the foresight to recognize the age wave and rise to its challenge. They are now paddling hard, intent on catching "the big one." When they respond with enthusiasm to the senior surge, they will experience the ride of their lives—reaching the older generation for Christ as never before and meeting human needs through the power of God's love.

3
Developing a Christian View of Life and Aging

It is just as important for anyone who ministers to and through older adults to develop an appropriate perspective on life and aging as it is for the seniors themselves. This chapter will focus on some issues that should frame the paradigm for an effective older adult ministry.

A *Christian* view of aging is far healthier than the traditional or secular one. A Christian view provides hope for today and anticipation for tomorrow. Because it answers basic questions concerning identity, it teaches us how to experience life fully, no matter what our age.

A secular view is given by sociologist Christopher Lasch when he writes, "Men and women begin to fear growing old before they even arrive at middle age. The so-called mid-life crisis presents itself as a realization that old age looms just around the corner. Americans experience the fortieth birthday as the beginning of the end. Even the prime of life thus comes to be overshadowed by the fear of what lies ahead."[1] This perspective results in destructive discrimination against older adults, which is coming to be known as "ageism."

Frequently, as I work in the area of older adult ministry, someone will ask me about my philosophy of aging. I usually answer that I don't really have one. Instead, what I have is a philosophy of *living*.

SOME FUNDAMENTAL QUESTIONS

There are three basic questions that provide an excellent way of developing or reevaluating one's philosophy of life: Who am I? Why am I here? Where am I going?

1. *Who am I?* This is a major question throughout life, but it takes on new meaning the older a person becomes, for it deals with both identity *and* purpose. Obviously, the response should go far beyond one's name or vocation. For me, this question has two answers: (1) my universal, shared identity; and (2) my unique, individual identity.

a. *My shared identity.* You and I share many points of identity with other Christian believers. The basis for this commonality is found in Scripture. For example:

"So God created man in his own image . . . male and female he created them" (Gen. 1:27). You and I are created in the image of God, as is every man, woman, and child who has ever lived. This means that we are more than the latest or highest in an evolutionary chain. We are not just another kind of animal. We are *human* beings—a unique order within God's creation—possessing body, mind, and spirit.

"For it is by grace you have been saved, through faith—and this not from yourselves, it is the gift of God. . . . Consequently, you are no longer foreigners and aliens, but fellow citizens with God's people and members of God's household" (Eph. 2:8, 19). We who are believers are also recipients of God's grace and members of Christ's Body, the Church.

"How great is the love the Father has lavished on us, that we should be called children of God! And that is what we are!" (1 John 3:1). We are loved by God, and because of that love, God calls us His children.

Closely related to "Who am I?" is *"Whose* am I?" This question is also helpful in defining your identity. It asks, "Who has ownership of your life and possessions?" This is not asking whether or not you're married or if you feel that your spouse or some other human being "owns" you. Instead, it is talking about God's claim on your life. If you have committed yourself to a faith relationship with Jesus Christ, the answer is clear: "You are not your own; you were bought at a price" (1 Cor. 6:19-20). God has redeemed us at high cost—the death of His Son—and because of that, you and I belong to Him.

Of course, modern secularists despise the idea of "belonging" to anyone other than themselves. In fact, any kind of commitment is seen as a limiting factor that deprives people of their entitled freedom.

However, as a believer, I do not find God's claim on my life to be at all troublesome. Because I am one of His children, my sense of belonging is not that of a slave to an autocratic master. My relationship is that of a child to his father. "Dear friends, now we are children of God" (1 John 3:2). And the basis for that relationship is love: "See what love the Father has given us, that we should be called children of God" (1 John 3:1, RSV). For me, that answers the "whose" question.

Who am I? Whose am I? Well, according to the Scriptures, I'm someone who is created in the image of God. And, through faith, I am the recipient of God's grace and a member of His family, the Church. I am loved by Him and am called one of His children. Finally, I am not my own; I am bought at a price, so I belong to God. These aspects of my identity I share with all Christian believers, and they give me a very wonderful sense of value and worth that has nothing to do with chronological age.

b. *My unique identity.* I also have an individual identity that belongs to me alone. You have one too. Each of us possesses an identity that is defined by our God-given gifts, talents, and resources. For this reason, none of us is exactly alike.

Paul tells us, "It was he who gave some to be apostles, some to be prophets, some to be evangelists, and some to be pastors and teachers, to prepare God's people for works of service, so that the body of Christ may be built up" (Eph. 4:11-12). Not every believer is an apostle or a prophet or an evangelist or a pastor or a teacher. But we all have God-given resources that give us unique and different identities.

Furthermore, because we are "not our own," our talents, gifts, and possessions bring with them a special kind of responsibility. God has entrusted these things to us so that we might glorify Him and benefit others. Consequently, we are to be stewards of our talents and resources, which has a significant bearing on the next question.

Did you notice that I did not use my vocation to define my identity? That's extremely important for anyone who is approaching retirement. If *who you are* is defined by *what you do,* you'll face a serious identity crisis the moment you retire. *Never allow yourself to be defined primarily by your vocation,* especially if you intend to retire from it. Remember, first and foremost, you are a much-loved child of God, a member of His royal family. Neither chronological age nor retirement can take that away from you.

2. *Why am I here?* Many elderly ask, "Why am I still here? Why hasn't God taken me? I am just a burden on others." These questions may be troublesome for many individuals, but Christians have the answer: "Therefore, I urge you, brothers, in view of God's mercy, to offer your bodies as living sacrifices, holy and pleasing to God—this is your spiritual act of worship" (Rom. 12:1).

For me, the answer to the "purpose" question is directly related to my answers to the "identity" question. Because God has given me love, I am motivated to respond. Because God has endowed me with certain unique gifts and talents, I feel compelled to use them in His service. Because I belong to God, I am called to be obedient to Him and do what He commands. I am called to serve and to be a good steward of my time, talents, and resources during my entire lifetime.

Mrs. Edith Carlson lives in a retirement home. Several years ago, she discovered that she has significantly more Bible knowledge than others in the facility. So, she has begun a once-a-week Bible study that is proving to be beneficial to her and others who attend. Mrs. Carlson is indeed obedient to the command to "go and make disciples of all nations" (Matt. 28:19).

Because of who I am and what I have been given, I believe my purpose is to participate in the fulfillment of Christ's primary purpose—to "go and make disciples." Christians call this the Great Commission. *Why am I here?* To love God and love others as myself. Jesus called this the greatest commandment (see Matt. 22:37-40).

But isn't age a factor here at all? Doesn't retirement mean God no longer has a purpose for my life? *I don't think so!* Somehow, I cannot believe that God placed me on earth to serve Him for just 65 years and spend the rest of my life in a rocking chair.

Dr. Donald McGavran, to whom we referred earlier, was a pioneer in the modern church growth movement. He did some of the most significant work of his long and illustrious career *after* he reached retirement age. Dr. McGavran used to say, "We don't retire as Christians. God never excludes us from His call to reach the world just because our hair is gray—or even if we have serious disabilities that limit the extent of our physical activity."

In fact, Dr. McGavran saw the senior years as a time of special opportunity for Christians: "When we reach the age where we are living under the shadow of death, we usually understand the marvelous truths of God's loving grace much better than younger Christians. I know so many of God's older children who have been so effective in reaching lost men and women for Christ. And some of them have even done this from hospital beds."[2]

We all know many people in our churches who have retired both from gainful employment and from active lay ministry. You've probably heard some of them say something like, "I've done my part; now it's up to someone else." Or, "My work for the church is finished; my commitment is over." Or, "Let

younger people do the work. I'm tired." This "rocking chair theology" deprives the church of the talents of many of its best
workers. (See chapter 4 for more on this.)

As Dr. McGavran kept insisting, "Our life doesn't end when
we retire. Our life goes on. We no longer have to work to earn
money enough to live on: but we can do all kinds of good things
that God wants done . . . there are so many people we can
counsel . . . there are so many people we can love! There's so
much change in the world that we can bring about if only we
will recognize that this is our task. This is the reason that we
have all the experience that we have had. This is the reason
why we were born!"[3]

Why am I here? I'm here to bring glory to God in every
way that I can. I'm also here to serve—to be involved in ministry, to use my gifts and other resources to the benefit of God's
kingdom during my brief pilgrimage on this earth.

3. *Where am I going?* The Christian answer to the "destiny" question is profoundly different from the secular answer.
Just before his death at age 92, Dr. McGavran answered the question this way: "To many people, death is simply the ending of life.
I, who was wide-awake yesterday, am dead today, and I will be
buried tomorrow. That's the belief of so many people. That's not
my belief—that's not my belief. I believe that when this body
dies, it's just like taking off an old garment. And I will be called
home to live in everlasting peace and joy and strength and glad-
ness with Jesus Christ my Savior . . . and with all my friends."[4]

Contrast that attitude toward life and death with the typical secular view. Most secular spokesmen contend that once we
have reached early adulthood, the "dying process" begins.
Some suggest that we actually begin dying the day we are born.
According to these views, our time is limited; our individual
cells begin a gradual process of deterioration from which there
is no escape. If our remaining years are seen as "downhill from
here," life's best is always past.

If *this* life is all there is, we might as well be self-centered
and hedonistic, devoting our efforts to pursuing maximum en-

joyment today—right here, right now! If the past is gone, and there is no future, then the present is all there is. So we "eat and drink, . . . for tomorrow we die!" (Isa. 22:13).

Indeed, for those who hold this prevalent secular view, life's final years become a cruel joke, merely prolonging and delaying the inevitable. Because growing old is a time to be feared, it seems far more satisfying to die young.

Of course, we who are Christians don't believe this at all!

THE BEST IS YET TO COME

The biblical perspective, with its belief in immortality, sees death and dying as only transitional—much like the "dying" in the ground of a seed, or the cocoon stage in the life of the caterpillar/butterfly. In this view, *the best is yet to come.* We can expect, in time, to turn in our infirm, handicapped, mortal bodies for liberated bodies that are free from sin, sickness, and death, bodies that are as different from our present physiques as a butterfly is from a caterpillar. Therefore, old age is not the coda to life's final strains but a prelude to life's next chapter.

The big difference for Christians is that *God* is the center of our existence, not *self.* We do not belong to ourselves. We have an eternal calling to pursue, individual assignments to complete. Our life's purpose is to follow and serve our Lord and Savior Jesus Christ. Life on this planet is not all there is. As one song puts it, "This world is not my home; / I'm just a passin' through."

As we Christians near the end of our present lives, we find ourselves identifying more and more with the attitude expressed by Paul in his letter to the Philippians: "For living to me means simply 'Christ', and if I die I should merely gain more of him. For me to go on living in this world may serve some good purpose. I should find it hard to make a choice. I am torn in two directions—on the one hand I long to leave this world and live with Christ, and that is obviously the best thing for me. Yet, on the other hand, it is probably more necessary for you that I should stay here on earth. Because I am sure of this, I know that I shall remain and continue to stand by you all, to help you forward in Christian living and to find increasing joy in your faith" (Phil. 1:21-25, PHILLIPS).

Or, as paraphrased by Kenneth Taylor: "For to me, *living means opportunities for Christ,* and dying—well, that's better yet! But if living will give me more opportunities to win people to Christ, then I really don't know which is better, to live or die!" (Phil. 1:21-22, TLB, emphasis added).

In many ways, life is like climbing a mountain—the higher we go, the tougher it gets. But the closer we come to the summit, the better our perspective. And the older we become, the more clearly we understand that this life is not all there is. We know, through faith, that for God's children there is a "prepared place," a heaven where death, sickness, and tears will forever be replaced by eternal peace, health, and happiness. That's where I'm going, and that's the basis of my Christian hope.

My philosophy is unaffected by aging! My life philosophy provides me with an understanding of my identity, my life's purpose, and my ultimate destiny. And it's a comfort to know that increasing chronological age has no effect other than to deepen my understanding of those profound life issues.

I will never be too old to lose the sense of value and worth that comes from knowing that I am created in the image of God, that I am loved by God, and that I am one of His children. This knowledge defines my life's purpose: to glorify and praise God and to serve Him. And I can do that regardless of age.

Nor will I ever be too old to face the difficult realities of this life with courage and hope, because I know where I'm going. It is this hope that brings a broad dimension to Christian believers, hope that imparts the necessary energy to imagine dreams, set goals, develop plans. As the philosopher Teilhard de Chardin has written, there is "no energy of despair . . . all conscious energy is . . . founded on hope."[5]

Hope is essential for all people, but especially for older adults. Vaclav Havel states, "Life without hope is an empty, boring, and useless life. I cannot imagine that I could strive for something if I did not carry hope in me. I am thankful to God for this gift. It is as big a gift as life itself."[6]

So, a philosophy of living and aging from a Christian perspective answers the questions, "Who am I?" "Why am I here?" "Where am I going?" Those answers provide a rich meaning to day-by-day living at any age.

4
Ageism—Is It Real in the Church?

Old age has its problems, but the wildly distorted image of old age may be the biggest problem of all. Fifty to 100 years ago, there would have been little need for this chapter because:

1. Prior to 1935, and the inauguration of our Social Security program, the concept of "retirement" was unknown. Before then, the chronological age of 65 had no special significance, and reaching it was not considered a milestone.

2. Most people died much younger than they do today. Only a few lived into their seventh and eighth decades. When Social Security was initially proposed, the average life expectancy was much less than 65 years. Few people were expected to live long enough to enjoy its benefits or to constitute a large enough group to have an impact on society.

3. Older adults were honored and respected because the wisdom of accumulated experience was valued.

Today, the facts and attitudes about "old age" have changed. Retirement has become a social and economic reality that, for most people, begins somewhere around the age of 65. Furthermore, people are living longer and better. On the average, Americans live 14 years longer than they did in 1930. Consequently, retirees are now the fastest-growing segment of our population. Yet, ironically, older adults are less honored and respected than before. On the contrary, they are often discriminated against and devalued.

THE NATURE AND CAUSES OF AGEISM

We live in a day when racism and sexism have been recognized as the unwholesome attitudes they are. Yet, unfortunately, ageism is alive and well—even in the church. Although it is no longer considered in good taste to make racist or sexist jokes, old age is still fair game.

Ageism is a pervasive, negative attitude toward aging and people who are growing old. Like racism or sexism, it is a destructive and discriminatory form of prejudice that is based on flawed stereotypes.

To a large extent, ageism is unique to our contemporary Western culture. For example, in much of Asia, where it is seen as a handicap to be young, ageism is virtually nonexistent. In China, it is believed that the older a person is, the more wisdom and knowledge he or she has. When asked, "How old are you?" a 55-year-old in China might cheat a bit and claim to be 59.

The majority of people in our society, including many in the church, are absorbed in a self-centered lifestyle, concerned only with the "here and now." There is little interest in the future or the past. Self-validation is based on looks, position, money, or power—attributes that often fade with time. The value of accumulated experience, which age brings with it, is often overlooked.

Social historian Christopher Lasch, in his book *The Culture of Narcissism,* suggests that narcissism may be one of the underlying causes of our culture's negative view of aging:

Our society notoriously finds little use for the elderly.

It defines them as useless, forces them to retire before they have exhausted their capacity for work, and reinforces their sense of superfluity at every opportunity. The fear of old age may stem from a rational realistic assessment of what happens to old people in an advanced industrial society . . . but it has its roots in irrational panic. The most obvious sign of this panic is that it appears in people's lives so prematurely.[1]

The greatest single cause of ageism is fear of growing old. A futureless view that *"this* life is all there is" results in hopeless feelings about old age and dying. The self-absorbed baby boom generation, which once proclaimed that "no one over 30 can be trusted," is a good example. Now in their 30s to 50s, its members often panic at the thought of growing old and thus search for "eternal youth." In so doing, baby boomers have unwittingly become active proponents of ageism, a "virus" that can infect us regardless of our chronological age.

A MATTER OF SELF-ESTEEM

In Rom. 12:2, the apostle Paul warns against conforming "to the pattern of this world." Whatever our age, most all of us have been squeezed and molded by the ageism that surrounds us. It affects not only our attitude toward others but also how we feel about ourselves.

Here are some questions to answer: Do you ever feel self-conscious about revealing your age to other people? Does the thought of growing old depress you? How paranoid are you about graying or thinning hair or noticeable wrinkles? Sometimes, ageism prompts us to try to look or act younger than we really are. (We've all done that, haven't we?)

Admittedly, it can be depressing to face up to our mortality. We begin life with what seems to be an almost inexhaustible supply of time. Then, all too soon, we notice that the days, months, and years are slipping by. As Bill Cosby's popular book title suggests: *Time Flies!* As it does, we may feel more and more uncomfortable about growing older.

The primary question is: How will you see *yourself* as you continue to grow older? Will you view yourself as a person of worth who is created in the image of God? Or as someone whose value depreciates with every birthday? We perpetuate ageism whenever we buy into the idea that growing older automatically diminishes our worth. Then, not only does our personal self-esteem take a nosedive, but we will allow conscious and unconscious prejudices toward older people in general to affect our thinking and behavior.

Ageism and the Church

Unfortunately, ageism afflicts more than our secular society. As more and more individual Christians become infected, the virus has begun spreading throughout the church. If the church is going to seize the opportunity of effectively ministering to senior adults, it will need to root out the ageism found in subtle ways in so many congregations.

In a society that places enormous value on youth-related attributes, there is a stigma attached to growing older. Even in the church, older adults—despite good physical and mental health—often feel inadequate and inferior, simply because they are older.

Is your church guilty of ageism? Consider these questions:

1. Does your church intentionally seek out young families without an equal outreach to older adults? *That's ageism!*

2. Does the membership see older adults as liabilities rather than assets? *That's ageism!*

3. How many persons in your church community are between the ages of 12 and 21? Do you have a pastor/leader assigned to this age-group? What percent of the church budget is spent on youth? In contrast, how many persons in your church are 55 or older? Do you have a pastor/leader assigned to this age-group? What responsibilities does he or she have beyond visitation of

the ill and homebound? What percent of the budget is spent on older adults? If a disproportionate amount of money, time, and staff is spent on youth, at the expense of effective ministry and outreach to older adults, *that's ageism!*

4. If your church were seeking a new pastor and had identified two candidates of equal qualifications and merit, would your church automatically choose the younger candidate? *That's ageism!*

5. What is your church doing to help its senior members prepare for effective living after they are no longer gainfully employed? The transition from the "fast lane" of full-time employment to the "slow lane" of retirement can be difficult, even traumatic. If your church is ignoring this issue, *that's ageism!*

6. How many key lay leadership positions in your church are filled by persons over 55? What is the attitude of younger church leaders toward older members? How do older members feel about themselves? Under-representation of seniors on church committees and boards may reflect negative evaluations of their capabilities. *That's ageism!*

7. Is your church offering its older adults opportunities to touch the lives of other people with the love of Jesus Christ? If older adults are not being used in evangelistic and teaching roles—maximizing their accumulated years of experience and knowledge—*that's ageism!*

Modern American society finds little use for older adults. It forces them to retire before they have exhausted their capacity for productive work, and then suggests that they occupy their time with hobbies or recreational activities. Unfortunately, the church follows society's lead. If our senior members are healthy, we entertain them; if they're ill, we visit them. All too often we see them as liabilities that deplete our energy, not as assets that can add vitality and know-how to our programs.

TWO VIEWS OF OLDER ADULT MINISTRY

Recently a pastor friend related to me how he had met monthly for lunch with the dozen or so retired members of his church. He was soon asked by younger leaders in his church whether this was really a "productive" expenditure of his time. This anecdote can serve as a reminder that there are two basic, but contrasting, attitudes regarding a congregation's senior members—and, therefore, two different ways to design a ministry to *and through* this group.

1. *Caretaking.* Even within the church, ageism is a destructive, prejudicial force that prevents many older adults from fully exercising their options or maximizing their God-given potential. It has been traditional to regard older church members primarily as "caretaking problems" requiring a large investment of pastoral time for hospital and shut-in visitation, grief counseling, and so on. Most activities for seniors are recreational and entertaining, usually with little emphasis on education or growth. In this view older members are considered a liability, a drain on the congregation's financial and staff resources—persons who take without giving.

This may have been an accurate assessment of older adult ministry in previous generations. And the church of Jesus Christ must always maintain a compassionate ministry for its family of believers, be they hospitalized or homebound people (of *any* age). However, in this closing decade of the 20th century, restricting the ministry for older adults to caretaking and recreational activities is both unrealistic and self-limiting for a church.

2. *Resource management.* As we have already noted, because of enormous changes that have taken place in terms of health and longevity, today's retirement-age adults are much more likely to be assets to the church than liabilities. For the most part, they are more intellectually alert and physically active than their parents and grandparents were at their age. Since, on the average, they can expect to live 10, 15, even 20 years longer than their counterparts of the past, a church's sen-

ior members have the potential to become one of its greatest resources for ministry and outreach.

"Rocking Chair Theology"

One almost universal barrier to older adult involvement in lay ministry is "rocking chair theology"—a voluntary withdrawal of retirement-age individuals from church-related activities. Unless your church is considerably different from the average, most of your older members have retired both from gainful employment and from active lay ministry. This not only robs seniors of the great joy of being productive and useful but diminishes a church's supply of available workers and the talents they might bring to its agenda.

Why do people act this way? Is it because they've actually worked themselves to the point of complete exhaustion and no longer have any energy left for further ministry? Perhaps in some cases. But, more often, the cause of "rocking chair theology" is our previously discussed enemy: ageism, combined with a worldly philosophy that sees retirement as a big "playpen."

Chances are that very few of your church's older members are confined to hospital beds or are homebound. Are they being enlisted for active duty? Or has the church banished them to self-enjoyment? Telling older adults they have "earned the right to take it easy" is a subtle form of ageism that encourages retirees to keep a low profile in the church. Would you be surprised to learn that the reason many older people say, "I've done my part; now it's up to someone else," is simply to avoid the embarrassment of being replaced or asked to step down. And what gave them the idea that they might no longer be needed? If you think the answer is "ageism," you're probably right.

Ageism is far more insidious than a prejudice that merely makes life less and less enjoyable for older individuals. Unchecked, it has the potential to destroy a church's vital intergenerational relationships.

There are no simple answers to removing the stigma of ageism. As with sexism and racism, we know it is not easy to stamp out negative stereotypes. But in the church—where the opportunity for mutual growth and development and support is not only encouraged but also commanded by Christ—we must accept the challenge to take a giant step forward, by redefining age as wealth and older persons as the truly rich among us. As Robert Browning once wrote, "Grow old along with me! / The best is yet to be . . ."

THE CHURCH'S RESPONSE TO THE SENIOR SURGE

How has the church been responding to the tremendous increase of older adults in our population? Of course, it will vary from denomination to denomination. Southern Baptists, for example, are miles ahead of most other groups in their work with seniors. Although some denominations have developed a system of retirement homes, they minister to only a very small percentage of church members. Other denominations have a senior department, but it is usually combined with other departments and given rather low priority. When one looks for an aggressive outreach program for older adults, it is very difficult to find in the structure of most denominations today.

Turning to the regional areas, one sees (in most cases) a small-scale replica of what the denomination is doing. Most regions have a committee that accepts senior adults as part of their responsibility.

What about the local church? When pastors are surveyed concerning their ministry for and with older adults, many respond, "We provide hearing aids in the pews." Or, "I include senior adults in my visitation schedule." To date, most local churches have not awakened to the opportunities and ministry potential in the present and future senior surge.

There is little doubt that the Body of Christ has in its very mission and biblical imperative the response possibilities for enlarged ministry. Most churches would acknowledge that there is no wholeness or wellness for a senior adult without the spiritual dimension, and they have the personnel, facilities, and organizational structure to address that need. Physical facilities, often empty most of the week, could be creatively used for ministry to seniors. A church also has organization—committees, boards, mailing lists, staff—that could be utilized if the desire were there.

So, with all the resources available, why isn't the church "leading the charge" and reaping the rewards of an effective ministry for senior adults? There are at least three reasons:

1. *Lack of vision and knowledge.* Some churches, pastors, and lay leaders do not have a clear understanding of what can and should be done. Without a vision, nothing will be accomplished, but dreams alone are not enough if church leaders have little or no training in the area of senior adult ministry. Sad to say, this is the case in tens of thousands of churches across America. Why is this? For one thing, very few seminaries have had courses about aging. Even if a pastor wanted to be knowledgeable in this field, he or she could find little help at a denominational seminary. The information and insights needed to be a successful pastor to older adults have been missing from most curricula until quite recently.

2. *Nongrowth excuses.* Another reason is inertia. In some churches, nongrowth excuses have gotten in the way of expanding the ministry. A nongrowth excuse is a reason, often an unsubstantiated opinion, why outreach to a specific group is considered impossible or undesirable. If such psychological barriers are not removed, they will inhibit growth and discourage those who are open to innovative breaks with tradition.

A nongrowth excuse often contains a small percentage of truth; but in its totality, it is only an excuse—a pretext to maintain the status quo. For example: "Our doors are open to everyone. Senior adults can attend whenever they want to. It is up to them." Or: "All those old people? We would soon have a reputation in the community as a dying church." Or: "The hope of our church is youth. That is where we need to focus." That second remark illustrates the infatuation some churches have had with youth. This can easily be seen by observing the energy, effort, personnel, and resources put into youth ministry, compared to other ministries in the church.

   3. *Self-imposed ageism.* Another growth-restricting obstacle is the attitude of many senior adults themselves. Plans for retirement are often based on a worldly philosophy of retirement that says, "We have served; now we want to be served." Many senior adults act like the rich fool in Scripture who said, "Take life easy; eat, drink and be merry" (Luke 12:19). Or, put in another way: "Let us go after all of our pleasures *now.*"

THE LAMENT OF A SENIOR ADULT

   As youth in the church, we were eagerly pursued. There were special programs, activities, camps, even a full-time youth director. There were parties, games, entertainment. And time moved on.

   As college-age youth, we had the church on a string. We were sought after for our music and as teachers and future leaders. However, only 10 of every 100 of us stayed in the same community. And time moved on.

   The church's welcome continued into our young adult lives. Its leaders were eager to have our young children attend Sunday School. We were candidates for every nominating committee and service opportunity. And time moved on.

   As middle-aged adults, we moved into the power structure of the church. We were asked for our financial support and influenced what others gave as well. We ran the church. And time moved on.

   Today, I am the same person I was as a youth with a few more wrinkles, but greater wisdom and experience. Though I am more spiritually mature, no one in the church seems to be interested in the leadership that I, or any of my peers, can offer. There are no special programs for us. There is no senior adult director, even though there are twice as many "white heads" in the congregation as anytime before and twice as many seniors as all the youth put together. Even the pastor, who tries hard, doesn't understand my problems. This is partly because our seminary, and hundreds like ours, doesn't teach what pastors need to know about my generation.

Yes, the pastor tries, but the age issues *he* struggles with I resolved 20 or 25 years ago. And even though my generation is the most faithful in worship and gives more than any other group in the church, we seem to be virtually ignored. Do you think that's fair? Is that the way the Body of Christ should function?

Well, we're not totally ignored. We regularly receive appeal letters from the denomination, the theological seminaries, and from our local church, asking to be included in our wills. But it will be many years before those wills take effect, for—in this age of extended longevity—we expect to live far longer than our parents.

What should I do with these years? I feel there is something I want to contribute, but I don't have the opportunity. God is not finished with me yet!

Should I look for a church that has a dynamic senior adult program? Or try to help my own church come alive in this area, even though there is a great deal of ageism to overcome? Maybe I should walk away from it all.

What would you do?

5

New Beginnings for Your Senior Adult Group

W hy do some senior adult groups grow with explosive life and vitality, attracting new members, seeing many come to Christ or renewed faith, and providing a real contribution to the growth and outreach of the entire church body—while other such groups are small and stagnant, cannot attract people, and generally have little or no role in the evangelistic growth of the church?

During the 1980s, considerable research and attention focused on the general decline of church membership that had plagued many denominations. As denominational executives and local pastors began learning and applying church growth theory, substantial new membership growth has been and continues to be realized. The insights developed and disseminated by such organizations as Church Growth, Inc. (Monrovia, California) have been greatly used by God for the growth of His Church, bringing a fresh breeze of hope and new life to increasing numbers of congregations.

But what about senior adults? Insights from the church growth movement have never before been systematically focused on the current problems and opportunities of reaching this population group. The remainder of this book is an important first look at some of the principles of church growth that relate directly to the older adult ministry of the church and can be applied with relative ease.

WHAT IS THE GOAL?

One of the fundamental differences between churches today that are growing and churches that are dormant is also observable in the senior adult groups in those churches. The difference can be summed up in one word: "purpose." The common ingredient in growing churches and growing senior adult groups is that their understood purpose is centered on a clearly defined goal of reaching out to unbelievers and bringing them to faith and Christian discipleship. By contrast, any group or church that exists primarily for the benefit of those persons who are already members tends to be characterized by stagnation or decline.

Purpose is the most important foundation for a growing senior adult ministry.

Scripture bears clear testimony that God's unswerving desire is for lost humanity to be redeemed and brought into His Church. Christ's birth, crucifixion, and resurrection opened a way of salvation so that all people might experience forgiveness of sin and reconciliation to God, finding new life in Christ as they become members of His Body, the Church. This primary purpose of God, which was proclaimed by Christ's disciples, is the motivation and power behind all growing churches . . . and growing senior adult programs.

Passage after passage in the New Testament clearly underscores God's intent that all will come to a knowledge of His redemptive love. The Book of Acts is the record of how those in the Early Church, in obedience to God's will, aligned themselves within this unswerving purpose—and the body of believers grew in numbers and influence during this era.

Perhaps the simplest statement of God's purpose is found in Christ's final words to His disciples: "All authority in heaven and on earth has been given to me. Therefore go and make disciples of all nations, baptizing them in the name of the Father and of the Son and of the Holy Spirit, and teaching them to obey everything I have commanded you" (Matt. 28:18-20). The Greek verb forms used in this passage give us further insight into the Lord's desire for His Church. The only *imperative* verb in Christ's command is "make disciples." The *helping* verbs— "go," "teaching," and "baptizing"—all amplify that goal.

Christ's entire life was mission-centered. He was *sent* by the Father to serve (Mark 10:45). His marching orders to His followers make it abundantly clear that He likewise conceived of His Church as mission-oriented: "As the Father has sent me, I am sending you" (John 20:21). Being Christ's disciples, therefore, requires commitment—above all else—to Christ's own mission to the world.

What does the Great Commission mean for the Universal Church—Christ's Body on earth? More specifically, what does it mean for the senior adult group in your church?

God's desire to accomplish His purpose is not adjusted according to the age of His servants. Scripture records that He called Abraham in his 75th year to be the leader of His people. Why didn't God call a younger person for this assignment? Was there something in the lifelong quality of Abraham that carried into his old age and qualified him for such leadership? Today there are many senior adults who have proven their abilities and are ready for the worthy purpose of communicating God's love to others and thereby furthering God's kingdom on earth.

Senior adult leaders concerned with being true to the Lord's desire for His Church are inevitably faced with this question: "Are the purpose and nature of our ministry accurately reflecting the mission of Christ?" This question must be examined at the local level before subsequent planning or activity will be of any consequence. Aligning the senior adult group's purpose with Christ's purpose is *the* crucial issue. This objective will be the primary foundation on which any effective group within the church will be built.

Perhaps the major difference between senior adult groups that are growing and those that are not growing is in their view of purpose. Whether specifically stated or subtly implied, every senior adult group has a philosophy of ministry—a reason to exist. Because this reason for being directs the focus of the ministry, it will determine how successful the church will be in reaching unchurched senior adults.

1. *Inward-focused groups.* In most nongrowing senior adult groups, the reason for being is exclusively a ministry to present members, those who are already Christians. While a concern for the spiritual health, personal growth, and social fellowship of those within the existing group is necessary, the reason many senior adult groups are declining is that these concerns have become their entire preoccupation and the focus of all activities.

What happens when priority is given exclusively to the nurture of existing members? Seniors in the church are urged to participate in the group because it will help them. The group is thought of as a refuge for intimate fellowship with other Christians, a personal and spiritual center where believers are nurtured to spiritual maturity. All programs, activities, and curricula reflect a self-limiting inward focus. This self-centeredness can be easily identified in the following statement of purpose we received from one local church: "We gather on a monthly basis to help older members grow spiritually and relationally. Involvement in the group will provide fellowship with other believers and support in times of need. Such involvement will be of benefit to everyone who participates."

There is nothing wrong with these important tasks if they are *parts* of the total ministry. But, in inward-focused senior adult groups, they become the *whole* emphasis and reveal an introverted concern for only their own members. Social activities are member-oriented, with little or no effort made to bring in non-Christians. Visitors often have difficulty crossing barriers of existing social relationships and exclusive traditions.

"Growth" of inward-focused senior groups, through reaching unchurched people in the community, is either not mentioned or is assumed to be an inevitable by-product of the group's activities. The truth is, however, that these activities do not motivate people for involvement in Christ's mission of reaching out to others. In fact, programming that is concerned with only the spiritual nourishment of present members creates a self-serving mentality that effectively seals off the group from the outside world.

Dr. Kenneth Van Wyk, who directed the educational ministry at the Crystal Cathedral (Garden Grove, California) for many years, underscores this point: "In my judgment, a nurture-oriented focus commits the serious error of making an end out of something that is meant to be a means. By definition it is self-centered and therefore suffers from a basic introversion. It violates the example given us in Christ's teaching and life, where ministry on behalf of others is central and primary."[1]

In most declining senior adult groups, the program, curriculum, activities, and training do not reflect the priority of outreach required by Christ and His Church. Further study shows that not only are such inward-focused groups a deterrent to growth but also often fail to reach the very goal intended: spiritual maturity for members. A senior adult group that is not concerned with or participating in the central purpose of fulfilling Christ's Great Commission to "make disciples" is actually stunting its own members' spiritual maturity and subverting the goal of developing Christlike qualities.

2. *Outward-focused groups.* The reason for being of most *growing* senior adult groups, by contrast, acknowledges a responsibility to the broader community. These outward-focused groups exist primarily to reach those not yet part of Christ's Body. And, as part of this purpose, they equip their members for ministry to those outside the church. While concern for the spiritual growth and nurture of existing Christians must be a crucial part of any ministry to seniors, outward-focused senior adult groups see this as a *means* to an end, not an end in itself.

In such senior adult groups, high priority is given to seeking, reaching, teaching, and discipling new people. The main focus of the organization's events, meetings, and curricula is outreach: *making disciples*. And the result is growth—for God gives the increase!

DEVELOPING A STATEMENT OF PURPOSE

A clear understanding of purpose is the most important starting point for a healthy and growing senior adult group. The purpose becomes the compass that provides direction and meaning for the group. For a Christian, a purpose is "worthy" when it relates to God's desire to reach lost humanity.

Unless such a purpose is established from the beginning, the senior adult group will soon degenerate into a self-serving, ingrown, closed-off, and visionless collection of individuals at cross-purposes. Attendance will tend to plateau or decline. Visitors will drop off, and the group will either die or remain small and impotent. The founder of A.A.R.P. understood the importance of a mission beyond oneself when she wrote into this organization's statement of purpose: "Not to be served, but to serve."

A good place to begin, when establishing a purpose for your group, is the Scriptures. In the Bible can be found marvelous models of "seniors" who have served the Lord. Consider the faithfulness of Abraham, the obedience of Moses, the fervor of Caleb, the piety of Anna.

Seniors in the Church of the Nazarene (Pasadena) discovered a verse from the Psalms that became their beacon and guiding motivation: "Even when I am old and gray, do not forsake me, O God, till I declare your power to the next generation, your might to all who are to come" (71:18). From this scripture, the group's leaders came to the conclusion that their ministry would be not only *to* seniors but *through* seniors as a source of inspiration to others. Their purpose—"to declare God's purpose to the next generation"—was to be achieved through activities that would encourage members to pray, to study God's Word, to have fellowship together, and to reach out to others with God's message of love and salvation.

Since the purpose statement of a senior adult group is the foundation upon which its programs should be built, it should:

- Unify the members of the group

- Provide motivation for involvement and a basis for accountability

- Give assurance that the group is doing God's work rather than just keeping busy

- Give the group an overall direction

- Define what the group will and will not do

- Give a basis for measuring accomplishments of the group

A good purpose statement has five basic components. To illustrate, consider the statement we developed for L.I.F.E. International:

Believing the call of God to make disciples is our greatest privilege and responsibility, it is our purpose to enhance the efforts of L.I.F.E. clubs, local churches, regional judicatories, and denominations in the task of disciple making, particularly as focused on senior adults.

To accomplish this purpose, we will disseminate proven concepts of senior ministry through seminars, study kits, books, videos, and other means and resources that facilitate worldwide the Great Commission (to make disciples) and the Great Commandment (to love), so that groups we serve may better achieve their full potential in making disciples.

The purpose statement for any Christian organization should include the following points:

1. *Biblical understanding*—what you believe God is calling you to be or do

2. *Target audience*—identifying those people and groups who are the focus of your ministry

3. *Major activities*—ways through which the Good News will be communicated

4. *Geographic area*—where you are called to minister

5. *Expected results*—what, with God's blessing, you anticipate

Developing such a statement for your senior adult group is time well spent. Then, once one is developed, *use it!* Use it in your group name. Use it in leadership and officer training. Use it in new member orientation. Use it in your newsletter. Use it in public prayers. Use it in lessons and Bible studies. Use it at social events. Use it to measure accomplishments. Use it and refer to it as often as possible.

In researching senior adult groups, we have found that many of them overlook purpose and begin with program. One such group has printed information on its activities that reads as follows:

> The Young 'N' Heart will meet each Thursday for a time of fellowship, food, and Bible study. The group comes together at 10:30 A.M. with an hour of fellowship. During this time of games, quizzes, skits, stunts, and shared memories the members will get to know each other better.
>
> A very important part of the meeting is the meal shared together. An elder's wife has organized nine teams of volunteer women to cook and serve the meal. Bible study follows. Overnight trips are planned twice a year, a short trip each month.

Notice how self-centered and inward-focused this group's priorities seem to be. Are sociability and entertainment its main reasons to exist? Another group's agenda follows a similar pattern:

> The regular meetings of the Prime Time organization are as follows: (1) Mature singles will meet the first Saturday of each month in the Family Life Center for a potluck fellowship and educational and recreational activities following the meal; (2) the entire Prime Time group will meet the second Saturday of the month for Game Day; (3) the entire Prime Time will meet each third Sunday of the month for a luncheon; (4) a group of the Prime Time ladies

will meet in the Family Life Center quilting room each Tuesday after Ladies' Bible Class.

It seems to me that the above program, while it may be of value, entirely misses the idea of *purpose*. Out of a statement of purpose, activities flow naturally and make sense to the members. When social or educational activities for the members are the only priority, a clear purpose seldom emerges.

Here is a suggested statement of purpose for a senior-adult group:

The _____ group has as its purpose to serve, not to be served. We believe God is calling us to take His love in concrete ways to the unchurched senior adults in our community, as well as to extend the love of God and the love of the family of God to those within the church. These goals will be accomplished through regular planned activities and emphases, with the anticipated result of God's blessing and people coming to Christ and the church. By-products of these activities will be spiritual growth, koinonia, social and recreational development.

SEEING THE POSSIBILITIES

Growing churches exhibit a common quality—they believe that their best days are still ahead. The same optimism is seen in growing senior adult groups.

Around every local church are pockets of older adults in desperate need of the gospel, people whose lives have a great void because they don't know Jesus Christ. The potential for reaching these individuals is amazing. Yet pastors and lay leaders who are not seeing such growth often ask, "Can it happen in *my* church?"

The answer to that question is in the affirmative. Yes, of course it can happen. The opportunity is there! And yes, there will be difficulties and setbacks, as there are when confronting any worthy challenge. But there is no reason your senior adult group will not grow if it is telling the Good News to needy people, if it is concerned about reaching out, if it is thinking and praying for growth. God wants His lost children found, and *His* power can transform "possibilities" into reality.

First you must believe that growth can occur. Too many senior groups have settled for too little. They have concluded, for varying reasons, that growth is quite impossible. So why work for it? That kind of pessimism is a self-fulfilling prophecy.

Why does that happen? Because many senior adult church leaders have become preoccupied with their own group. They like their group and their friends. That's perfectly natural. But the outsiders remain outsiders. And there is no way of reaching those outsiders unless the present membership and its leaders broaden their view of purpose to include those not yet part of the group.

6

Target-Group Evangelism

Any congregation that desires significant evangelistic gains and membership growth in the church of tomorrow will need to become effective at what we call target-group evangelism. This strategy identifies a specific segment of society (or "people group") and then systematically researches, communicates with, and builds bridges to persons in that group.

There are hundreds of target groups in America. In recent years the baby boomers are probably the most publicized, but there are myriads more—plenty to go around for all churches. Among the potential targets for evangelism available to most churches is an extremely receptive and growing group that can be easily identified and focused upon. Because of its nature and size, it offers an unusual opportunity for ministry and growth for nearly any church. This, of course, is the senior adult population.

As we have seen, the entire Western world has suddenly found itself in the midst of an age wave, or senior surge. While the media and marketers trumpeted the baby boom generation, huge numbers of Americans moved into their 50s, 60s, and 70s. Today, social scientists (and astute church leaders) are coming to recognize the vast significance of this overlooked and rapidly growing generation. For the church leader, the important questions are: "Is this group really receptive? And how can we structure effective outreach to this group?"

THE RECEPTIVITY OF SENIOR ADULTS

Donald McGavran, one of the founders of the modern church growth movement, observed a remarkable phenomenon on the mission field of India 50 years ago. He noted that when Christianity flourished in a particular area or region, it was often because entire villages or groups of people came to faith in a short period of time. During these "people movements," as he later called them, entire castes and tribes would become Christians.

Dr. McGavran also observed that although some tribes and castes of people were, at certain times, more *receptive* to the gospel, other groups tended to be *resistant*. His subsequent recommendation to missionaries who desired to see the Christian harvest in great numbers was to seek out receptive people groups—people whom God had prepared—and focus evangelistic strategy in that direction.

This principle of receptivity is just as relevant today as ever. And senior adults are a people group particularly receptive to the Good News. Here are three reasons why, and the implications for your church:

1. *Seniors are experiencing many changes in life.* You may be familiar with the Holmes-Rahe Stress Scale developed by two physicians from the University of Washington. These men identified the various changes in life situations that people experience and ranked them in order of severity or intensity of stress. The researchers then examined the effect of these transition events by determining the probability that persons experiencing them would later be hospitalized. Finding a strong cor-

relation between the two factors, they concluded that stressful life events often result in debilitating physical symptoms.

A subsequent study[1] took this same stress scale and looked for a relationship between these transition events and a change in religious lifestyle—specifically moving from an unchurched lifestyle to Christian faith. The conclusion was that people tended to become active church members much more often during times of transition. When people's traditional points of reference change, they seem more inclined to make other changes in their lives as well.

An important insight here is that on the Holmes-Rahe Stress Scale, over half of the events typically occur in the lives of persons over age 50! The older people become, the more frequently they experience life-changing events. These events provide windows of opportunity for the church in that people seem to move from resistance or indifference to the gospel to receptivity to its message of hope and salvation. Another way of seeing these events is as experiences used by the Holy Spirit to open people's eyes to needs that cannot be filled in human terms.

Figure 3 is a modified version of the Holmes-Rahe Stress Scale we have developed to integrate additional life events that often occur among senior adults.

FIGURE 3. ARN-MODIFIED SENIOR STRESS SCALE

Adult Age Life Event	Rank
1. Death of a spouse	100
2. Divorce	73
3. Move to retirement home	70
4. Marital separation	65
5. Death of a close family member	63
6. Major physical problems	53
7. Marriage	50
8. Realization of no meaningful faith for eternity	47
9. Financial loss of retirement money	47
10. Forced early retirement	46

11. Unable to maintain driver's license   45
12. Marital reconciliation   45
13. Retirement   45
14. Spouse confined to retirement home   45
15. Change of health of family member   44
16. Gain a new family member   39
17. Death of a close friend   37
18. Difficulty in getting medical insurance   36
19. Change in number of arguments with spouse   35
20. Mortgage over $100,000   31
21. Foreclosure of mortgage or loan   30
22. Feelings of not being needed   29
23. Feelings of lack of purpose   28
24. Outstanding personal achievement   28
25. Wife begins or stops work   26
26. Revision of personal habits   24
27. Significantly less contact with the church   24
28. Significantly decreased contact with children/friends 25
29. Trouble with the boss   23
30. Minor physical problems   20
31. Change in recreation   19
32. Change in church activities   19
33. Change in social activities   18
34. Mortgage or loan less than $100,000   17
35. Change in sleeping habits   16
36. Change in number of family get-togethers   15
37. Change in eating habits   15
38. Vacation   13
39. Christmas   12
40. Minor law violation   11

One of the best ways to show that the Christian faith and the church community provide a relevant response to issues older adults face is to plan a senior ministry around some of these transition events. For example, I was recently conducting a seminar in a Lutheran church. Across the hall, at the same time, the church was holding a support-group meeting for people who had suffered a stroke. There were over 20 persons in the group, only a few of whom had previously been involved in the church.

A Baptist pastor from Washington told me recently of his church's Crisis Deployment Team, made up of members who are specially trained in helping persons deal with the loss of a spouse or other loved one. All the members involved had personal experience in this transition event. It has been an effective way for this church to provide tangible expression of Christ's healing love and thereby see many come to faith and church involvement. The pastor also told me that the helping process had serendipitously helped those on the crisis team deal with their own sense of loss and grief.

2. *Older adults have an increased desire for meaningful relationships with others.* For those seniors who are able to provide comfortably for themselves, their next most important need is people. Of course, at all ages we need relationships to provide us with a sense of belonging, affirm our self-worth, and give us a chance to love and be loved in return. We satisfy this need in many ways—through family, friends, career, and participation in community activities. However, these human contacts become gradually less available to seniors. Children leave home to pursue their own careers, parents become infirm or die, old friends move away. Retirement can also increase an older adult's feeling of isolation, for it not only severs ties with former work associates but is often a reason to relocate to new and unfamiliar surroundings. Meaningful relationships are therapeutic and may contribute to longevity. One research physician from Johns Hopkins University calls loneliness the No. 1 killer, "Some other illness goes on the death certificate, but the prime cause was loneliness."[2]

Churches where love is intentionally taught and practiced will attract people—particularly senior adults. Over 100 United Methodist churches in Nebraska recently completed a coordinated 13-week study/application titled "Growing in Love: Seven Steps to Becoming a More Loving Person."[3] According to Robert Folkers, then chairman of evangelism for the Methodist churches in Nebraska, "This study was a significant experience for all those involved, but I particularly noticed a high involvement level among our older adults. They took to it like a duck to water."

In the video *Live Long and Love It!* a new Christian describes his journey of faith after retirement:

> I'm not really sure whether I was an agnostic or not, but I was always so busy making a living that I had no time for going to church or for thinking about God. But when I retired I entered the most difficult time of my entire life. Although I never became truly suicidal, the thought of ending it all did cross my mind more than once.

> And then my neighbor, who was also retired, made an intentional effort to be my friend. He was kind and caring and I soon found myself trusting him. My friend belonged to a kind of support group for retired people which met at a church, and he invited me to attend. Although I had serious misgivings about church and Christians, I went with him.

> It wasn't at all what I expected. I found a group of people who also were struggling with the difficulties of retirement. And despite my being a virtual pagan, they accepted me. They offered me "no strings attached" love and support at a time when I needed it most.

> Well, today I'm no longer a pagan. God is real in my life—and my only regret is that I didn't find out about God's love sooner. Now I'm committed to sharing with as many people as I can what's happened to me. And that gives me a real sense of purpose. I've never been happier.[4]

3. *Senior adults want (and need) to make a meaningful contribution to society.* Some authorities suggest that life can be broken into three basic periods:

- *Through age 25—preparation/experimentation:* defining oneself through acquiring individual values, education, a unique self-image. Priorities in this period of life tend to be self-centered.
- *From age 25 to age 65—productivity:* defining oneself through career, material acquisitions, marriage, family. Priorities in this period of life tend to focus on financial security.
- *Age 66 and over—redefinition:* defining oneself through family or vocation is no longer relevant. Priorities in this period of life tend to focus on finding meaningful activity and a sense of purpose.

Not all seniors consciously recognize their need for redefinition, but many discover an elixir for good physical and psychological health because they have found new ways to answer the basic questions of "Who am I? Why am I here? Where am I going?" (see chapter 3). In contrast, it is common for those who have not successfully redefined their personal purpose and identity to experience mental and physical deterioration.

Social and psychological experts today agree with the timeless prescription for sound health and long life: "Those who *get* the most are those who *give* the most." Or, as Christ said, "Whoever wants to save his life will lose it, but whoever loses his life for me will find it" (Matt. 16:25). Churches with growing senior adult ministries take the biblical theme of ministry seriously, extending it to senior adults in particular. "A mere cycle of games, trips, entertainment, and handcrafts wears thin," says Mark Bergmann, a noted authority on aging. "Helping others to play games, taking others on trips, entertaining others, and making handcrafts for others, these activities give the dimension and provide the setting for the discovery of meaning."[5]

Nowhere in the Bible does it say that Christians retire from discipleship and service at age 65! Billy Graham recently said, when asked about his plans for retirement, "I wasn't aware that Christians retire from ministry."

WHY IS THE CHURCH MISSING THE MARK?

Why aren't more senior adults being reached with the gospel of Jesus Christ and becoming responsible church members? One might think that, because many congregations are already composed of a considerable number and percentage of older adults, evangelism and additional growth among this age-group would be an easy process. Not true! In fact, we have apparently been unsuccessful for some time in effectively evangelizing older adults. The graph below is just one of several studies that indicate that few people who are Christians today came to their faith during their later years.[6]

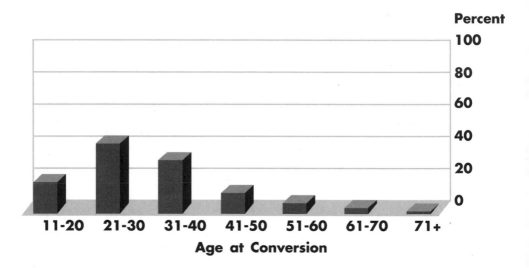

1. The church's outreach emphases have traditionally focused on youth and young adults. In research conducted in 500 churches, we found that 8 out of 10 churches had youth directors (volunteer or paid), but only 1 in 95 had a senior adult director! This overallocation of staff and dollars for youth deserves a closer analysis of stewardship and "return on investment."

- Only 1 in 10 participants in the average church youth group will be an active member of the same church 10 years later.

- The youth department typicality *requires* resources (time, effort, money, people) of a church, rather than being a source of resources for the church.

- The loyalty of young people to a particular church is usually shallow—if/when a successful youth pastor leaves and is not immediately replaced, the youth leave as well.

In comparison:

- Senior adults have more time available for volunteer activities, including church ministries.

- Senior adults typically have the largest amount of discretionary funds of any age-group and financially support the causes and institutions they believe in.

- Senior adults tend to be less transient and stay in the same church for longer periods of time.

Certainly it is important to have an effective youth outreach strategy. Energy needs to be spent on providing an excellent and attractive ministry for young people. But it is equally important to have an effective senior outreach strategy. Churches should emphasize both. Unfortunately, *ageism* (discrimination against older adults) occurs in many churches and limits those churches' potential for growth. It is time for a more balanced emphasis.

2. When approaching older adults, a church is dealing with "seasoned consumers." By the time a person is 50, he or she has heard a wide variety of sales pitches, including those from religious marketers. Most seniors have developed a skepticism that looks through the froth and fluff often connected with evangelistic appeals. Whatever the product or message, older adults are informed and wary shoppers.

For example, I recently bought a new car. My old one had over 100,000 miles and was no longer reliable. Its replacement was not the first new car I ever purchased. In fact, in my driving career, I have owned 14 different cars, so I was not a beginner at this. I began with a trip to the library where I checked on cars in *Consumer's Guide*. Then I studied the "Blue Book."

What was the markup a dealer added, and what could I expect as a discount? What did it tell me of the trade-in value of my present car? With this background, I was able to focus on the kind of car I wanted and what I could expect to pay. Next, I began to call dealers that carried the make of car I had decided on. After my phoning, I decided to visit three dealers. This gave me the opportunity to compare what each one had to offer. The final result: I secured a car that I am quite satisfied with, at a competitive price that I felt made it a good deal.

The business world is beginning to see the senior market as one that needs to be approached in a particular way. For example, senior buyers place a high value on quality that can be demonstrated and on reliable and friendly service. Because older adults want to be in control of their own lives, they usually base their decisions on facts and experience, not emotions. The church that wants to minister to senior adults effectively will need to understand *who* they are: their goals and motives and needs.

3. A third reason the church is not reaching more seniors is that it is using old, inappropriate paradigms. A church that replaces propositional evangelism with genuine love and caring will see greater results as a by-product of that Christian love. To help churches be effective in ministry to senior adults, we have encouraged churches to form L.I.F.E. clubs (Living in Full Effectiveness). Each club is provided a standard of excellence— guidelines and goals for effective ministry. One of the standards is that a L.I.F.E. club shall have a love/outreach project suitable for its situation, designed to build relationships with older adults not presently in the club or church.

4. A fourth reason for the weak ministry to and with older adults is that churches seldom have an organizational structure that facilitates evangelism to this age-group. In many churches, the only senior adult ministry is a small Sunday School class or a mission group, either of which may have been in existence for such a long time that it has inadvertently closed itself off to newcomers and visitors. When soon-to-be-retired church members don't find anything appealing in the existing senior adult

ministry, they just walk away and say, "No thanks. I'm not ready to be associated with those people yet." Visitors in the same age-group will have an aversion to *any* church involvement if lackluster programs are the only kind available.

Compare this to a church with an active senior adult ministry that sponsors a monthly banquet with special themes, speakers, music, where 8 to 12 percent are visitors. Such churches have an effective structure to contact and incorporate people into their groups. In so doing, effective evangelism occurs.

GETTING STARTED

The "graying" of America could be the growing of the church. In most congregations, the possibilities for an outreach-oriented, growth-producing program for seniors are tremendous. For reasons we have already discussed, senior adults are as a whole particularly receptive to the gospel. While there are many seniors already in the church, there are hundreds of thousands waiting outside. An effective older adult ministry is an imperative for any church dedicated to proclaiming the gospel and carrying out the Great Commission.

How can your church start or enhance its senior adult ministry? Here are a few suggestions (more will follow in later chapters):

1. Begin by identifying the people 55 years and above in your own church and in your community. Develop a profile of both groups, including "Age Groupings," "Needs," "Interests," "Family Status," "Marital Status," "Mobility and Physical Conditions," "Skills, Interests, Hobbies."

2. Plan a three-month trial program with and through seniors to assess interests, participation, and opportunities for ministry.

3. Raise the awareness of your entire membership to this opportunity for ministry and the church's specific response. Plan a Celebration of Seniors Sunday. Show the

video *Live Long and Love It!*[r] which challenges the entire congregation to adopt an attitude and lifestyle that will carry them to a rich and full life at *any* age.

4. Begin looking for a full- or part-time pastor for senior adults. In most churches, there are *twice* as many adults over 55 as youth from 13 to 20 years! This unique opportunity certainly merits focus by a special staff person.

There is no question that the decade preceding the 21st century will be critical to the health of the church in America, but the church is not even keeping up with national population growth. As secularism continues to sweep across the nation, the church must gather its full resources for a strategic struggle.

Jesus said, "Look at the fields! They are ripe for harvest" (John 4:35). Senior adults can be reached and discipled in significant numbers by most churches. And, as one pastor told us, "It may well be our—and their—last opportunity."

Are you and your church ready for the senior surge?

PART TWO

~ ~ ~

Applying Growth Principles to Senior Adult Ministries

~ ~ ~

7
Practice *Oikos* Evangelism

L et us share with you a timeless secret of growth. Because understanding and applying this idea in your senior adult group will result in tremendous outreach to new people, it is a key characteristic of any healthy and growing group. It is called *"oikos* evangelism."

OIKOS IN THE EARLY CHURCH

This growth principle actually dates back to the first century and is the model that Christ gave to His disciples. The term *oikos* is the Greek word for "household," and in evangelism it refers to a strategy of identifying webs or networks of believers. The same idea can be used to target the unchurched friends and relatives of present members as the prime source of prospects for your senior adult group.

Examples from the New Testament indicate that *oikos* evangelism was common as the early faith spread:

- In Luke 8:39, Christ told the demoniac to return to his *home* and describe the great things that God had done for him.

- In Luke 19:9, Zacchaeus was told by Jesus that salvation had come to his *house.*

- John 4:53 describes how the royal official's entire *household* believed, following the healing of his son.

- In Acts 10, we read how Cornelius (whose entire family or *household,* was God-fearing) had a vision, and sent for Peter. When Peter arrived, Cornelius "called together his relatives and close friends" (v. 24).

- In Acts 18:8, Luke describes how Crispus (the leader of the synagogue at Corinth) and his entire *household* believed in the Lord.

- In Acts 16:12-15, Luke describes how Lydia, in Philippi, believed in the Lord and was baptized with members of her *household.* Later, in that same city, the Philippian jailer believed, as did "his whole family" (v. 34).

- In 1 Cor. 1:16, we read that Paul baptized the *household* of Stephanas.

In addition to these direct references to the *oikos* of believers during the rapid spread of the faith, there are numerous passages where this "webs principle" of growth is seen in practice:

- Mark 2:14-15 describes how Jesus called Matthew (Levi), the tax collector; soon after, many *other* tax collectors were dining with Jesus and following Him.

- Luke 7:37—8:3 recounts how a sinful woman was forgiven and that soon *other* grateful women gave their support to Jesus.

- Luke 15 describes a man who found his lost sheep and called his *friends and neighbors* together to rejoice. In the same chapter, Jesus tells of a woman who found a lost coin and rejoiced with her *friends.* Finally, there was a joyful reunion of *friends* to celebrate the return of the lost son to his father's home.

- John 1:40-42 records that Andrew brought Simon Peter, his *brother,* to Christ.

- John 1:44-45 tells how Philip brought his *friend* Nathanael to Christ.

Author Michael Green observes that the New Testament Church adhered to the strategy of using the household *(oikos)* in the Christian advance.[1] The early Christians knew that when the Good News was heard and demonstrated by friends and family who were known and trusted, barriers to unbelief were removed and receptivity to the gospel increased tremendously.

WEBS IN TODAY'S CHURCH

Webs of kinship (the extended family), community (friends and neighbors), and shared interests (associates, work relationships, recreational contacts) are still the paths most people follow in becoming Christians today. Here are some simple yet profound reasons why *oikos* evangelism should be a major part of any senior adult ministry's growth strategy:

1. It is the *natural* way that senior adult groups grow.
2. It is the most *cost-effective* way to reach new people.
3. It is the most *fruitful* way to win new people.
4. It provides a constantly enlarging *source of contacts.*
5. It brings the greatest *satisfaction* to members.
6. It results in the most effective *assimilation* of new members.
7. It tends to win *entire families.*
8. It uses existing *relationships.*

Research conducted by Church Growth, Inc., on why people first come to Christ and His Church provides astonishing support of the *oikos* strategy of growth and outreach. Over 40,000 laypeople were asked the question, "What was responsible for your coming to Christ and this church?" The answers varied, but they generally fell into eight categories. The percentages for each category are summarized below:

Special Need	2%
Walk-In	3%
Pastor	6%
Visitation	1%
Sunday School	5%
Evangelistic Crusade	½ of 1%
Program	3%
Friend/Relative	79%

Growth in the Free Methodist Church in Bellingham, Washington, is a typical example of the "webs principle" in operation. The pastor has kept records of the networks that have contributed to church growth through outreach to new people. One web that is still growing started with a young man named Ron Johnson [last names have been changed]. Figures 4 through 7 show how it grew.

FIGURE 4. STAGE ONE OF RON JOHNSON'S WEB

RON JOHNSON
28 yrs.

Ken, Mary Morris
31, 29 yrs.

—Cousin—

FIGURE 5. STAGE TWO OF RON JOHNSON'S WEB

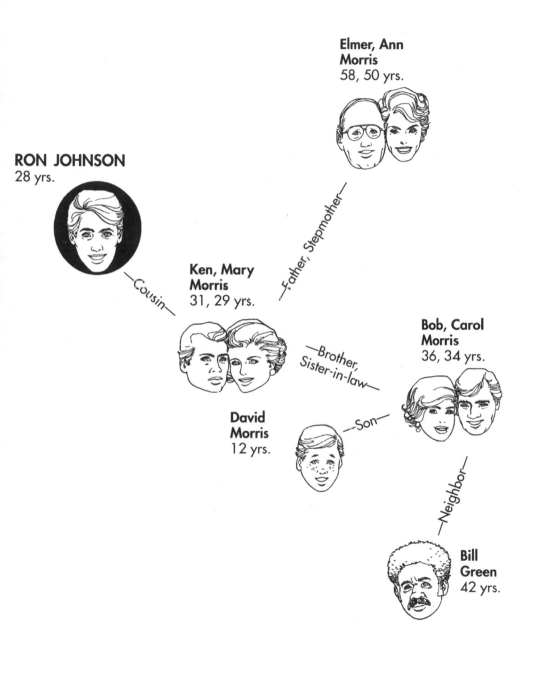

Elmer, Ann Morris
58, 50 yrs.

RON JOHNSON
28 yrs.

—Cousin—

Ken, Mary Morris
31, 29 yrs.

—Father, Stepmother—

—Brother, Sister-in-law—

Bob, Carol Morris
36, 34 yrs.

David Morris
12 yrs.

—Son—

—Neighbor—

Bill Green
42 yrs.

FIGURE 6. STAGE THREE OF RON JOHNSON'S WEB

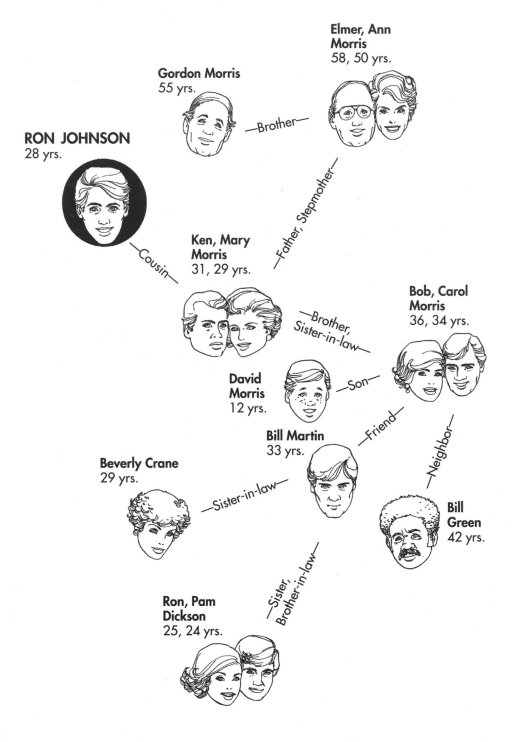

FIGURE 7. STAGE FOUR OF RON JOHNSON'S WEB

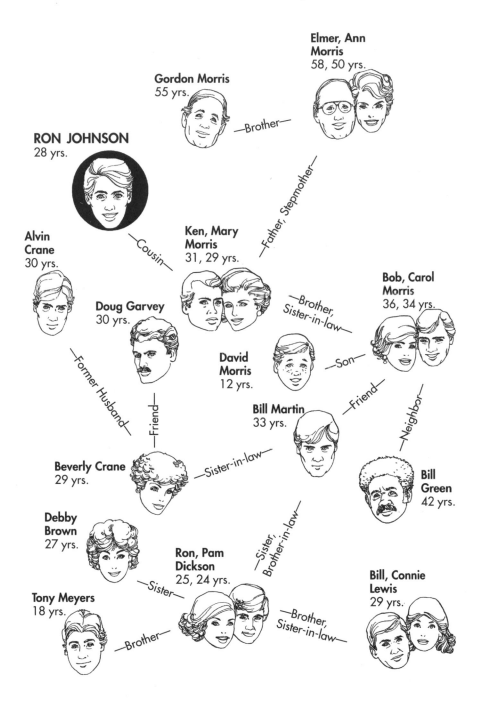

FIGURE 8. STAGE ONE OF MARLENE BOSTROM'S WEB

A second web was traced in the church. It, too, continues to grow today, as illustrated in figures 8 through 11.

USING *OIKOS* EVANGELISM IN YOUR SENIOR ADULT GROUP

The fact that a great majority of people come to Christ and the local church through webs of relationships has great implications for your senior adult group. The following seven strategies—each of which uses "webbing," or *oikos* evangelism—are important keys to moving your group forward. These strategies can be applied by any group desiring to be obedient to Christ's command to "go and make disciples."

FIGURE 9. STAGE TWO OF MARLENE BOSTROM'S WEB

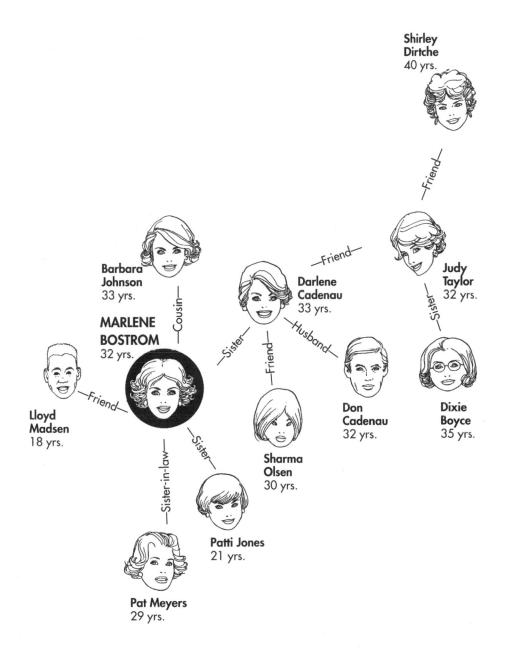

FIGURE 10. STAGE THREE OF MARLENE BOSTROM'S WEB

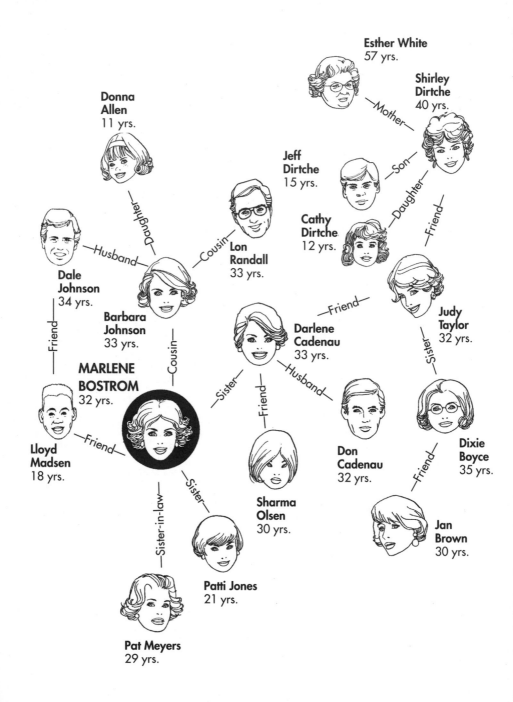

FIGURE 11. STAGE FOUR OF MARLENE BOSTROM'S WEB

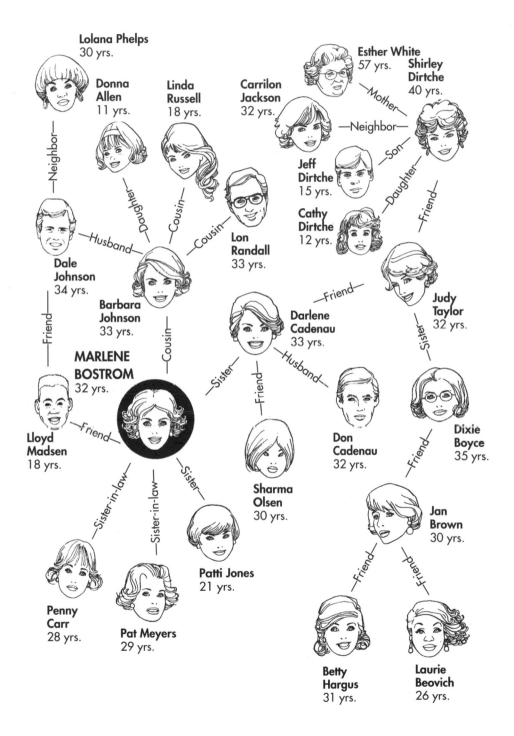

FIGURE 12. GROWTH POTENTIAL WITHIN VARIOUS WEB RELATIONSHIPS

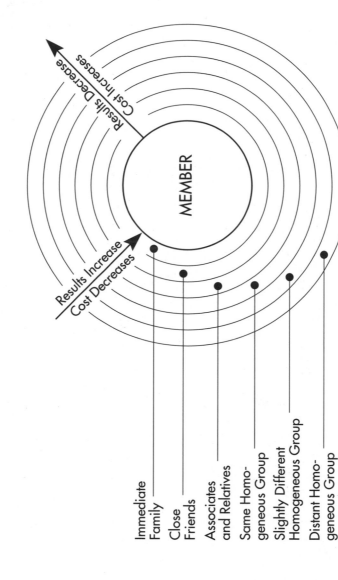

Results Decrease
Cost Increases

Results Increase
Cost Decreases

MEMBER

Immediate
Family

Close
Friends

Associates
and Relatives

Same Homo-
geneous Group

Slightly Different
Homogeneous Group

Distant Homo-
geneous Group

Strategy 1—Design growth around webs of relationships. Webs are social ties between people. They represent immediate and extended family ties, relationships within special-interest or work-related groups, and the bonding between friends and neighbors. The people most responsive to your senior outreach efforts and most likely to be added to your church will be found within the webs of members presently in the group. When a new person comes into your group, it does more than add one additional person to the roster. It opens a brand-new, untapped web of prospects: the person's friends and family now outside the church. A senior adult group—indeed, an entire church— that seeks growth should be enormously interested in all such webs. Figure 12 is a diagram of how this works.

Strategy 2—Identify unreached people in the webs of present members. In researching unreached people, Robert Orr analyzed the membership of a variety of churches. He discovered that, on the average, each member had 8.4 unchurched contacts in his or her web of influence. In congregations where most members had been Christians for a long period of time, that average dropped to approximately 4 contacts per member. In congregations with a large number of new Christians, the figure was 12. Similar research was done by Rev. Wayne McDill with a sampling of Southern Baptist churches in Texas. His findings were identical.[2]

Enormous growth possibilities are presently available to most senior adult groups if they build a prospect list based on these webs. A group of 15 persons, for example, could easily compile a list of 60 to 100 potential new members. Figure 13 is an illustration of where these prospects may be found.

The next step is to personalize your approach to these potential new members. For example, the First United Methodist Church of Anderson, Indiana, has established a "caring system" that was designed to respond to the particular needs of each person on its prospect list. As individuals or families are identified, a Caring Committee develops a profile on the interests, needs, or special problems each person is facing, along with the ways

FIGURE 13. POTENTIAL SOURCES OF GROWTH

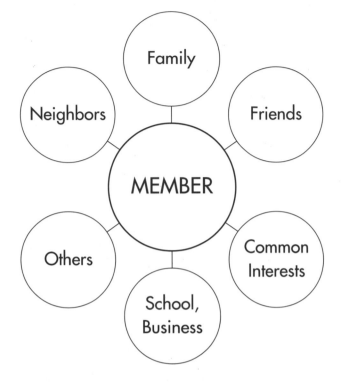

the church might best respond. The church then plans a strategy for contacting each family and/or individual, inviting them to participate in a specific group or activity of the church. Each active member in the congregation is seen as a resource to help make this "caring system" work. Compiling a list of prospects, along with devising a strategy for each prospect, is a proven way to growth in either the church or a senior adult group.

Strategy 3—Disciple to the fringes. Let's suppose you are the leader of a senior adult group of 25 people. In your group is Mary Smith. If we assume that Mary is typical, she has 8 relatives, friends, and associates who are not presently in Christ or the church. A diagram of Mary's list of immediate prospects would look like figure 14.

Next assume that six months after Mary identified these people, she has been instrumental in seeing 3 others—Bill, Jane,

FIGURE 14. MARY SMITH'S WEB OF INFLUENCE

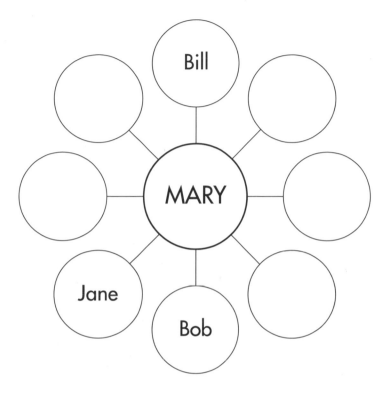

and Bob—make a Christian commitment and become members of the church and the senior adult group. Now "discipling to the fringes" begins to take place. Mary's original web of 8 people has enlarged to include the webs of Bill, Jane, and Bob—adding another 10 individuals to the prospect list (see figure 15).

Bridges have been built from Mary to a growing number of prospects, including those in Bill's, Jane's, and Bob's webs of influence. Yet, the possibilities are virtually unlimited, for radiating outward from Mary's 8 initial contacts are other webs of accessible people who could be added to the prospect list (see figure 16).

It was precisely this expanding pattern of outreach that caused the New Testament Church to explode. *Oikos* evangelism continues to be the most natural and effective means of reaching people today. However, it is not enough just to know about this principle. Specific strategies, plans, and procedures must be established to follow relationship webs to the fringes, discipling more and more men and women in the process. Of course, not everyone will be reached, but there is no more re-

FIGURE 15. SECOND STAGE OF MARY'S WEB

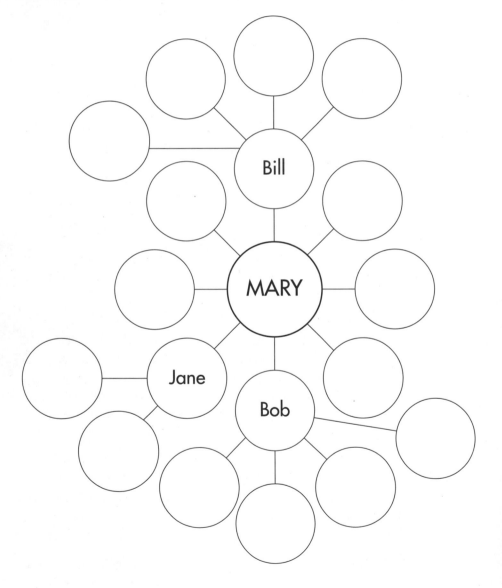

FIGURE 16. MULTIPLYING THE EFFECTS OF DISCIPLING

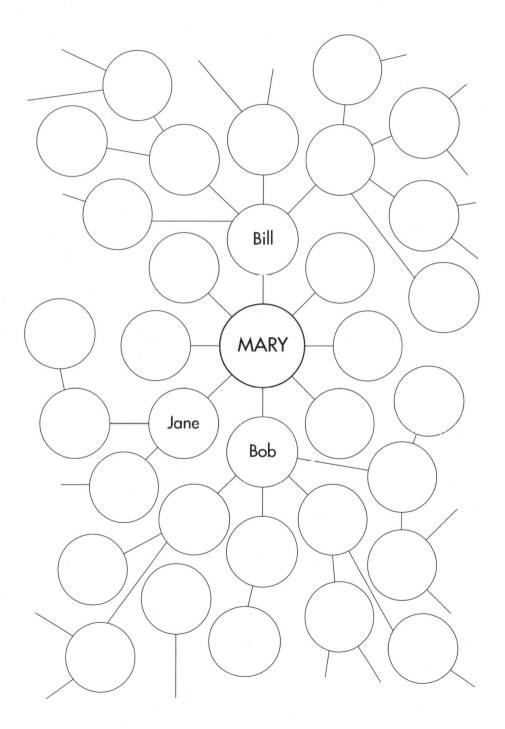

ceptive "soil" available than the people in these webs. When they are identified and focused on, the harvest will be great.

Strategy 4—Utilize recent converts. This strategy emphasizes the importance of using new Christians to accomplish further growth. Recent converts open doors often closed to established members. Figure 17 illustrates a natural phenomenon that occurs in every church and church-related senior group. The circle represents the church. The pyramid represents the world. The person at the bottom of the pyramid represents a person in the world but outside the Body of Believers.

When a person becomes a new Christian and church member, he or she still has a large number of friends and other con-

FIGURE 17. THE PYRAMID OF BELIEVERS

Active Church
Leader

Getting More
Involved

Growing
in Grace

Regular
Attender

New
Christian

Non-
Christian

Church

World

tacts in the world. As time passes, however, the maturing Christian maintains fewer and fewer contacts in the world and more and more relationships within the church. The reason is simply that a Christian feels more comfortable associating with other Christians. His or her new life in Christ is less compatible with the lifestyle of people outside the church. Because growing senior adult groups recognize that recent converts have a great many more contacts with unchurched prospects than do long-time members, they find ways to train these new believers to share their faith with their friends and family.

Strategy 5—Build new webs. From our discussion of Strategy 4, recall that when left to natural patterns, longtime Christians maintain fewer and fewer contacts with nonbelievers. Does this mean that they are absolved of their responsibility to reach new people? Of course not. But it does mean that a deliberate strategy of building new webs must be set in operation.

A growing senior adult group will develop creative ways to build new webs by which present members can reach people outside the church. One example of how this principle can work has been provided by the Carmel United Methodist Church in Carmel, Indiana. This church has developed a successful strategy of identifying and reaching out to people who move into its ministry area. Members are held responsible for an area two blocks around their homes and are always on the lookout for newcomers to the neighborhood. Members are encouraged to immediately introduce themselves to their new neighbors, invite them to dinner, cultivate their friendship, and be alert to ways the church and its groups respond to these people's needs.

Strategy 6—Pray for unreached individuals. There is power in prayer! Constant, earnest prayer is vital for the growth of the church and any senior adult group. That means not simply vague utterances for "a more Christian world" or "a return to our Christian heritage," but a sincere, fervent petitioning of God for specific individuals who are outside Christ. We must pray for people who are in our webs of influence, asking that those we name might be reached and discipled into the Body of Christ.

Scripture abounds with promises that if we but ask in Jesus' name, He will hear and answer. Any senior adult group thrives when prayer is directed toward specific individuals it wants to reach.

Grace Baptist Church of Newhall, California, discovered this important principle. Following weeks of preparation, planning, and prayer, members of the church were asked to list on a card the non-Christian friends and relatives for whom they would pray during the coming year. On one Communion Sunday morning, members put these cards on the altar as a symbol of the covenant they had made with God to reach those people. The staff distributed the names to individual prayer groups, so they were prayed for regularly by other church members. From the initial prospect list of over 800 names, 276 have found Christ as Lord and Savior, and every month the church is baptizing new people and welcoming them into the fellowship.

Understanding the principle of webs is an important concept for senior adult group leaders and all members of your church. Identifying and evangelizing those webs is a proven and effective way to turn potential members into comrades of the Cross.

8
Incorporate Newcomers

We have asked hundreds of people from various churches to describe something positive about their church. Almost invariably, the answer is: "We are a friendly church."

People like to think of their church as "friendly," and indeed many of them are. But in most cases the people are friendly only to each other, not to visitors. This truth was dramatically brought home to Dr. Carol Pierskalla, who describes attending church services regularly; sometimes even visiting more than one church on a given Sunday.[1] While she found the "greeters" were friendly, as were the pastor and members of the congregation, she says, "Never did anyone contact me on a one-to-one basis to reach out and explore the possibilities of a potential friendship or to ask if I had some need that they could help with." No one called or visited her after she had taken the initiative of visiting the church.

"Why is it," she asked herself, "that we in the church do not do a better job of caring about the strangers that are within our gates?"

This situation could be duplicated thousands of times in churches across America. But it does not—and should not—have to be that way. In churches with growing senior ministries, there is a high priority on welcoming and involving newcomers. An effective senior adult group is concerned about outreach and assimilation.

THE SENIOR ADULT GROUP: AN EFFECTIVE RESOURCE FOR INCORPORATION

Let's first look at four reasons why a senior adult group is so well qualified to incorporate new people.

1. *The senior adult group can build bridges of friendships and relationships.* Friendship is the most important key in binding visitors and new members together and establishing their loyalty to the church. The stronger and more valued these relationships, the more assured you can be that newcomers will be actively involved on a continuing basis.

In one research study, church dropouts were asked two questions: (1) "Why did you drop out?" and (2) "What would most influence your returning?" The answer regularly given to question No. 1 was, "I did not feel part of the group." The majority response to question No. 2 was, "The friendliness of the people."[2]

2. *The senior adult group expands the opportunities for role involvement.* There is a direct relationship between the number of new people a church can incorporate and the number of roles and service opportunities that exist. A church with a large number of responsibilities to be filled by laypeople will assimilate a much greater percentage of new members than a church with a large number of members but few opportunities for participation.

What kinds of roles and tasks might the senior adult group provide? The possibilities are vast. There are opportunities to serve on committees (planning, social, welcome, evangelism, etc.). There are regular duties (making announcements, taking attendance, serving as a greeter or song leader or missions coordinator). When a person is involved in a personally meaning-ful task, he or she is quite likely to become an active member of the group and the church.

3. *The senior adult group is able to monitor involvement levels and respond when needed.* One of the best barometers for predicting a person's future participation in church activities is his or her involvement in a small group within that church. When people become regular and active group members, regular worship attendance usually follows directly. But when a person's attendance in a small group begins to fluctuate, it often is the first of several steps out the back door of the church. A senior adult group that keeps attendance records can take the steps needed to bring a "drifter" back to secure moorings.

4. *The senior adult group provides a basis for fellowship.* An effective group can provide the strength that comes from mutual love, support, and encouragement. The spiritual cama-raderie of fellow Christians, wrestling with mutual problems and seeking to learn and grow together, makes this group a highly effective instrument for incorporating new people into the church.

Principles of Incorporation

There are four principles of incorporation that are particu-larly applicable to a senior adult group.

1. *An effective senior adult group builds an incorporation consciousness.* Because a strong emphasis on incorporation within the group is the first step in an effective outreach strate-gy, the goal of adding and assimilating new people must be giv-en high priority and visibility. The active involvement of new members and visitors must be a major agenda item at every meeting. Success should be measured not only by how many newcomers attend but also by how many become functioning, active parts of the group and therefore have a reason to stay.

Here are some suggestions for raising an incorporation consciousness:

- Establish a lay committee whose responsibility is to oversee the welcome of newcomers and their level of participation during the first nine months of their life in the group or church. The committee keeps accurate records and updates information on every new member or prospect. It responds with a note or phone call when signs of inactivity are observed.

- Create new roles and opportunities for service. Endeavor to match newcomers' interests, gifts, and skills with involvement in the group. If no appropriate roles exist, create them.

- Interview once-active but now inactive members to determine why they dropped out. Lessons learned from these people are valuable in alleviating potential problems for other members.

2. *An effective senior adult group encourages homogeneous subgroupings within the larger heterogeneous group.* When only one type of senior adult group is offered, the church is inadvertently saying, "You are all the same." But senior adults are not all alike. Over the years, they have developed unique interests, goals, spiritual needs, and friendships that often make them quite different from others in their age-group. To ignore the unique characteristics of people is to overlook one of the most important keys to effective incorporation. Senior adult ministries that sponsor subgroups that meet at different times and are tailored to a variety of needs and interests are much more likely to assimilate newcomers into active involvement.

3. *An effective senior adult group knows its saturation point.* Every group has a "saturation point" beyond which it cannot grow. The Southern Baptists on the basis of considerable study of their Sunday Schools suggest setting class enrollment ceilings for every youth, adult, and senior adult class. When that attendance figure is reached, a new class is immediately started.[3]

Peter Wagner, a church growth researcher, studied the groups in the Lake Avenue Congregational Church and found an interesting phenomenon. In plotting the attendance of adult groups in this 3,000-member church, he observed that growth occurred up to a certain numerical point. When the growth line passed this level, attendance became erratic and soon began to drop. When a group later began to grow again, it increased only until it approached its apparent "saturation point." Then attendance dropped off again.[4]

Determining the maximum growth potential of your senior adult group(s) is important. Here is how: Plot the growth pattern of each group. If you see a size beyond which growth seems to hesitate or stop, you have begun to identify a group's saturation level. When attendance in the group begins approaching that level, it is a clear signal to organize a new group.

4. *An effective senior adult group makes a conscious effort to be open to newcomers.* Sociologists know that long-established groups can easily become closed to outsiders. The longer any group has been in existence, the more difficult it is for a newcomer to break in. The more traditions and experiences that members hold in common, the harder it is for outsiders to identify with the group's agenda. Keeping the group open to new people is a continuing job, and it does not happen automatically.

9

Establish a Small-Group Network

Healthy senior adult ministries sponsor more than one group. In fact, the more subgroups that exist for persons age 55 or older within the ministry, the healthier will be the life of the overall ministry for seniors. A small-group network encourages growth because it can usually provide significant benefits to existing and prospective members more effectively than a large heterogeneous organization.

1. *Small groups provide pastoral care of members.* Experiencing healing for the hurts that all of us encounter in life is one of the great benefits of being a member of a local church. However, in some churches the personal caring function occurs only through the pastor or a staff person. When this happens, the number of persons to whom the church can minister decreases sharply. Pastors can seldom be effective caregivers when the ratio of pastoral staff to active members exceeds 1:150. However, when a small-group network is established, the sharing and supporting role of Christ's Body is much stronger and can touch the lives of more people.

2. *Small groups assimilate newcomers and facilitate active church involvement.* Research indicates that people remain active in a church when they have friends in that church. Participation in a small group is one of the best ways to build and strengthen such relationships. This will be particularly true in a senior adult ministry when the small groups are structured around one or more shared qualities (such as interests, marital status, recreation, needs). Newcomers and visitors will more easily become "insiders" if they can develop friendships in a common-interest group where they feel at home.

3. *Small groups keep people from dropping out.* Senior adults involved in small groups in the church are much more likely to remain active than those who are not part of a small group. Again, research indicates the importance of relationships in the growth of any church-related group. When people who have dropped out of active church involvement are surveyed, the primary reason given for their inactivity is: "I didn't feel wanted, loved, or cared for. I didn't feel like I belonged." Involvement in a small group is perhaps the best way an older adult ministry can provide that sense of caring and belonging.

4. *Small groups help older adults grow spiritually.* Every small group, regardless of its purpose or goal, should have a commitment to seeing its members grow in their spiritual life journey. As members of the group study, learn, question, and grow together, they help each other expand their spiritual depth and breadth.

5. *Small groups reach a larger number of older adults.* Particularly when new small groups are started, experience and research indicate that new people will be attracted. As we will see later in this chapter, groups can and should be started around a variety of functions. Whether it is a recreational group, a study group, or a service group, the presence of newly established groups has been shown to be a magnet for involving people who had not been previously active in the larger group or the church.

CHARACTERISTICS AND TYPES OF SMALL GROUPS

To qualify as a small group, and thus provide the benefits listed above, each of the following characteristics must be found:

- The group must meet at least once a month, preferably two to four times a month.
- The number of people participating in the group must be between 3 and 15. Having any fewer than 3 or any more than 15 generally frustrates the function and purpose of a small group.
- Each member must feel needed and wanted and an important contributor to the success of the group.

One key to enhancing the effectiveness of your senior adult ministry is to realize that the *kinds* of small groups you have is much less important than the fact that you have such groups and are regularly starting new ones. Most of the benefits that small groups bring to a ministry will occur regardless of what kinds of groups they are. Nevertheless, the groups you start do need to be based on known qualities of the people you are presently in contact with, and those to whom you intend to reach out. There are five basic types of groups, each of which is described below.

1. *Covenant groups.* These groups have the primary purpose of building caring and intimate relationships among members. They tend to require relatively long-term commitments for members, anywhere from six months to two years. The group may decide to take breaks from their meeting schedule (Christmas season, summer, etc.), but there is an understood covenant between members to be regular and active participants. Covenant groups usually range in size between 4 and 12 members. They tend to be made up of people who have one or more qualities in common, such as similar ages, marital or family status, interests, occupations, hobbies, concerns. Because friendship ties are frequently based on homogeneous characteristics, one of the benefits reported by members of covenant groups is the strong bond of commonality they feel.

2. *Study groups.* Unlike covenant groups, these study groups focus more specifically on a predetermined topic. As a result, they tend to attract people of similar interests, even though members may be a mixture of age, race, marital status, or economic level. Study groups usually focus on a book or a theme, and they are usually of shorter term than covenant groups—often six to eight weeks, though they may choose to continue meeting beyond that point. These groups will attract people who might shy away from involvement in a group that requires a longer or higher commitment. They are especially helpful for people whose schedule frequently changes and/or those who may have previously had a negative group experience.

3. *Outreach groups.* These are groups that intentionally seek to involve unchurched people. An outreach group is usually topic-oriented, focusing on issues of interest or concern to its present and prospective members. The subjects may be on such varied topics as "parenting," "healing of family relationships," "Who is Jesus?" "justice," or stretch as far as the imagination might lead. The key is that the topics address relevant issues and provide meaningful benefits to those who participate. Outreach groups usually require no time commitment, may vary in size, and often meet on "neutral turf" (somewhere other than the church facility).

4. *Action groups.* The focus of these groups is on the accomplishment of a specific task, as people come together to address a particular need they see in their church or their community. A group's meeting may involve prayer for direction, research on the extent of a need, and discussion on how best to fill it. Then members go to work and perhaps enlist others in the actual project. Examples of action group agendas include door-to-door demographic canvassing, planning and producing a dramatic play of community interest, working with youth on developing a coffeehouse ministry, organizing and staffing a book table for a community street fair, opening a health-care clinic staffed by volunteer health professionals, or researching church and community needs for a daycare center.

5. *Support groups.* These groups exist primarily to provide emotional and spiritual support for their members. While not evangelistic per se, their spiritual emphasis often plants seeds in nonchurched individuals that bear fruit later. Occasionally these groups are led by church professionals within their area of expertise, using a book as a point of reference. Group programs usually last 8 to 12 weeks. Meetings may consist of lecture, discussion, or a combination of both, depending on the leader. The size of a support group is often more than 12 people, although it may break into smaller, more manageable groups for discussion periods. Since they tend to be larger than other "small groups," support groups often meet in rooms such as the church fellowship hall. Examples of people to whom these groups bring support, encouragement, and healing are widows/widowers, single parents, cancer victims and their families, the unemployed, and drug or alcohol abusers.

Figure 18 on pages 112-13 is a "group grid" constructed by Karen Hurston.[1] It lists the many types of groups that can exist in a church setting and compares them as to objective, characteristics, styles, strengths, and weaknesses. This chart is also applicable to smaller groups within a senior adult ministry and are therefore worth studying if you are planning to establish a small-group network for seniors in your church.

How Many Small Groups Are Enough?

How many small groups should your older adult ministry have? One? Three? Five? Here is an easy method to determine how many groups are appropriate for your church:

1. Determine the number of persons in your church who are 50 years and older.

2. Subtract the number of persons who are already actively involved in a small group.

3. Add 25 percent to this number (to anticipate and allow for nonchurched persons).

4. Divide this number by seven (the average size of a small

FIGURE 18. HURSTON GROUP GRID

TYPES OF GROUPS	FOCUS/ OBJECTIVE	SECONDARY CHARACTERISTICS	DIFFERENT STYLES	STRENGTHS	WEAKNESSES
BIBLE STUDY GROUP	Objective: To learn what Scriptures say Focus: On biblical truth	Usually studies focus on books of the Bible, on topical subjects, specific passages, or books on Christian living—led by a single teacher or moderator	Discussion, "musical" teachers, exposition, in-depth study, devotional, informational	1. Develops a rational basis for beliefs 2. Provides structure for individual study 3. Creates appreciation for revealed truth 4. Helps set criteria for Christian living 5. Provides thought for continued application	1. Provides information separate from the crucible of living Has idea of salvation through education 2. Has idea of salvation through education 3. Words become the focus—not action
PRAYER GROUP	Objective: To agree together in prayer Focus: Toward God or others outside group	Usually there is the expectation that God will do what one asks	Conversational, topical, circle, intercessor	1. Trains people to deal with God directly 2. Develops an attitude that God cares about us 3. Creates an awareness of the working power of God 4. Keeps a person open to hear God's voice	1. Limits personal interaction between participants 2. Eliminates those who are not in a good place spiritually 3. Supports instead of trains those who lack social skills
FELLOW-SHIP GROUP	Focus: Development of relationships	Needs solid foundation for deep levels of trust and openness; intimacy and accountability are needed.	Care groups, koinonia, age groupings, kinships	1. Fosters "cell" activity 2. Warm, accepting environment 3. Tends to be more homogeneous and comfortable 4. Focuses on change in the individual	1. Lack of definite purpose 2. Has tendency to turn into a social time 3. Can become a clique
SOCIAL GROUP	Focus: Social interaction	Varies in size and type of people involved. Can be divided into age, personal interests, or a combination. Not regular—can be a one-time event.	Picnics, holiday focus, special interest, camping/sports	1. Provides open nonthreatening atmosphere 2. Can function without a trained leader 3. Satisfies surface needs	1. Event oriented with a short life-span 2. Shallow relationships 3. Nonconfrontive to the inner person

	Focus / Objective	Description	Components		
TASK GROUP	Focus: On specific projects	Gathers people to a specific function to create an environment to get work accomplished	Evangelism, social concern, building project, seminars, committees	1. Gives people a sense of vision 2. Provides a place for those who lack in social skills 3. Strong feeling of togetherness 4. All are participants	1. Small percentage of church involved 2. Personal needs are not welcomed 3. Self-righteous attitudes crop up and hinder
ACCOUNTABILITY GROUP	Focus: To give others permission to hold one another responsible for one's walk with Christ Objective: Discipleship	Can study Bible or a book about Christian living with emphasis on responsible application	Components: 1. Discussion 2. Study 3. Prayer 4. Confrontation	1. Further development of responsible discipleship 2. Focus on application 3. Helps set criteria for Christian living in supportive atmosphere. 4. Challenges one to grow	1. Too intense for some to handle 2. Can seem to put too much value on performance 3. Must be careful not to dominate, but to encourage
COVENANT GROUP	Objective: To be obedient to Christ Focus: Combines functions of other groups	These mixed pattern groups usually end up focused more on one or two components.	Components: 1. Bible study 2. Sharing 3. Prayer 4. Focus or discipleship	1. Allows for a variety of activities to take place 2. Place to grow in Christian maturity and ministry 3. Good place to share needs and learn how to apply the Bible 4. Allows for openness	1. Usually ends up with focus on one component 2. Group can take itself too seriously
HOUSE CHURCH	Objective: To worship, learn, minister, and grow together	Group of 15 to 50 who gather on a regular basis and do most of the functions of a church service. Worship is considered important and financial giving is involved.	Some use of Scripture, participatory involvement in prayer, high priority to worship	1. Creates atmosphere of excitement, praise, thanks 2. Supportive climate for involvement 3. Inclusion of worship tends to comfort 4. Since format similar to church, many easily adapt	1. Can seem too much a repeat of what church is already doing 2. Financial stewardship can create tension 3. Can try to do so many things that no one task is done well

group). The result will give you a good idea of the number of small groups you should plan to have for an effective senior adult ministry.

The viability of the small-group network in a senior adult ministry depends on another statistic: the number of groups that have been started in the last two years. This measurement is important because all groups tend to grow introverted over time and seal themselves off to outsiders. Because of this natural phenomenon, a senior adult ministry should be regularly starting new groups that allow newcomers to become involved immediately, rather than trying to break into an already established group.

A good rule of thumb is that one of every five groups should have been started within the past two years. To calculate this, begin by determining the number of small groups that presently exist in your church for persons 50 years and over. Next, divide that number by five.

The resulting number will tell you how many small groups should have been started in the past two years, and therefore whether you are providing an adequate number of new groups to accommodate newcomers.

SUGGESTIONS ON FORMING SMALL GROUPS

1. *Decide on the purpose of each group.* An effective senior adult ministry will have a number of groups, so that any person inside or outside the church over 50 years of age will have the opportunity to find a group that is right for him or her. Keep in mind that people will tend to become part of and stay active in groups that are an extension of their present interests, needs, and/or desires. Researching the kinds of groups that reflect these concerns will be an important part of a successful small-group network.

2. *Recruit leaders with matching vision for the groups.* While professional training is not necessary to be a small-group leader, a vision for the purpose and people involved is essential.

Look for people in your membership who are, in the words of Rev. Bob Stone of Hillcrest Chapel in Bellingham, Washington: "F.F.A.T."—Faithful, Flexible, Available, and Teachable. If a person has a heart and desire for service, the skills of leading a small group can be taught. (There are a number of excellent resources available for teaching group leaders. One such publication is *The Small Group Leaders Training Course* by Judy Hamlin, available from Church Growth, Inc., P.O. Box 541, Monrovia, CA 91016.)

3. *Meet with and train leaders.* The purpose of a group will define the training that will be necessary. If you intend to have many different groups, you may first want to meet with each kind of leader separately. Weekend retreats or six- to eight-week teaching sessions are two of the best ways to accomplish training. Leaders should receive clear-cut instruction on the purpose or mission of the group and how to measure progress against that goal; facilitating social and interpersonal dynamics; resources available to the group; methods of member recruitment; and communication channels available to group leaders if questions or problems arise. One goal of leadership training should be to build a dynamic among group leaders so they feel they have a support group of their own. It is also important for a pastor to have regular communication with group leaders and revise plans on the basis of this feedback.

This chapter has presented some highlights on the subject of small groups in your senior adult ministry. There are a number of helpful books, resources, and seminars available on this topic. Our suggestion is that you continue to develop your knowledge of the important ingredients for small-group networks.[2] As you do, you will find that you are attracting and involving more and more people from both inside and outside the church. And you will be well on your way to an effective extension of your church's ministry to adults over 50 years of age.

10

Stimulate Spiritual Growth

~~~

K
athleen Fischer hit the nail squarely on the head
when she wrote:

>Thanks to research in the field of aging, we
now better understand many of the physical,
psychological, social, and economic aspects of the aging
process. But we have not yet fully answered the deeper
questions emerging from our longer life expectancy. Is this
lengthening of human life an anomalous triumph of science
and technology over purpose and meaning? Does anyone
know how to live the last years meaningfully and joyfully?

>It is precisely here that the need for a spiritual per-
spective is most acutely felt. Since the spiritual is inter-
woven with all other aspects of life, we cannot fully treat
human aging without attention to this dimension, especially where meaning is concerned. In fact, we cannot really
understand *any* stage of our life journey unless we can
penetrate the mystery of its final stage.[1]

Building a "spiritual perspective," especially among senior
adults, is a new frontier for those concerned with improving the
quality of life. In the majority of writings in the field of geron-

tology, "God" is seldom, if ever, mentioned. In my own experience as a patient in the hospital, while recovering from a stroke, I found the doctors and therapists to be helpful, but there was no one with the slightest understanding of how the resources of faith could be applied toward recovery.

I am an A.A.R.P. member, and I encourage all senior adults to be part of this fine organization. However, at a recent national convention that my wife, son, and I attended, we never heard the word *spirituality* or any reference to God, even though we attended almost every session and workshop. The only exception was at the conclusion of the convention, when the new officers were sworn in and asked to repeat, "So help me God."

Stimulating spiritual growth should be of major importance to all senior adult leaders. In fact, that challenge is being addressed in almost every *effective* older adult ministry.

WHAT IS "SPIRITUALITY"?

For a Christian, "spirituality" goes beyond familiarity with biblical truths and stories, although that plays a part in developing faith. Nor is spiritual maturity measured by attendance at church services or a church-related group, although that, too, is important. Rather, it is an affirmation that all life has its foundation firmly fixed in the cement of God's truth, power, and grace. Spirituality was modeled by Jesus Christ in His command to "love the Lord your God with all your heart and with all your soul and with all your mind . . . [and] love your neighbor as yourself" (Matt. 22:37, 39). It is in this all-embracing concept that we see true spirituality lived and expressed.

Who could question the importance of a strong spiritual dimension in one's life? At stake is the ability to live our remaining years meaningfully—and walk to death's door with faith and hope because we make claim to the resurrection of Jesus Christ.

Abraham Maslow, a noted psychologist, gave to the world a helpful tool in his now well-known "hierarchy of needs." Maslow's thesis was that human life can progress from its lowest, physiological level to its highest dimension: self-actualization. While he didn't relate the concept to aging or to religion, it is easy to see how this progression fits the idea of enlarging the inner life, the life of the spirit. The Christian's route to self-actualization is salvation, which implies wholeness. It is by affirming our redemption through Jesus Christ that we discover our significance in God's universe.

When we begin to see the process of growing older as an ascending rather than a descending journey, new horizons begin to open. With such a view we do not yearn for what used to be. Instead, we seek ways of harvesting the experiences of a lifetime so that the flowering of that life might bring forth new beauty. This desire for deeper meaning usually surfaces in midlife, as we wonder, "Why am I here?" (see chapter 3). Because spiritual maturity helps us discover our true purpose in life, it allows us to welcome aging as a natural progression of changes by which we attain the highest level of human experience.

But how is a senior adult to achieve this self-actualization? Because he or she is dealing with the life of the spirit, it is the responsibility of the church to lead the way. But first its clergy will need to catch up with the issues and the opportunities!

ENCOURAGING SPIRITUALITY

With few exceptions, church professionals have received little or no training to deal with the spiritual maturation process, nor how to be models for helping others develop and enlarge the inner life. Yet, encouraging spirituality should be one of the primary goals of any specialized ministry for older adults.

The First Church of the Nazarene of Pasadena, California, has wholeheartedly accepted this challenge. The senior adult group—the Forerunners—builds into its programming those activities they believe will encourage life in the Spirit, or spirituality. For example, here are some of their activities:

1. *Early Christians.* Each Friday morning at 6 A.M. seniors meet with younger believers to praise God and cover church-

wide needs with prayer. This group has been called the "central heating system" of the church. The group has met for the last 23 years, using a format of singing, a short devotion, covering a large chalkboard with praises and petitions, and hearty praying. They model the religious life of early Christians.

2. *Prayer and fasting.* Each Tuesday at noon, about 20 seniors meet in the chapel to fast and have an old-fashioned prayer meeting. This ministry involves testimony, singing, and at least 40 minutes of intercessory prayer.

3. *Prayer warriors.* About 35 seniors receive a weekly list of prayer requests from members of the church family. These volunteers, including many shut-ins, have committed themselves to pray *daily* for each prayer request.

4. *Sunday morning prayer team.* Each Sunday morning, a number of seniors gather in the chapel to pray for the worship service, including the pastor, the choir, the worship leaders, and the entire congregation.

5. *Attending Sunday worship.* The Forerunners ministry encourages seniors to attend worship services with a spirit of anticipation—bringing Bibles, entering the sanctuary reverently, sitting where they can fully participate in the service, and singing with joy.

Once a year, Forerunners lead the worship service. Some seniors read Scripture, others lead prayers or sing in the choir, which includes 60 Forerunners. Taped testimonies are sent to homebound seniors who can no longer attend regularly, letting them know that their church has not forgotten them and values their participation.

Forerunners conduct worship services in four different convalescent homes once a month. Several retired pastors assist in preaching and leading music for these outside services.

Other spiritual enrichment activities of this senior adult group are less formal. Although they, too, promote Christian fellowship, the focus is on maintaining ties with *all* members of the congregation through ongoing support systems.

1. *Walk-and-talk devotional exercise.* When the weather is warm, about 25 Forerunners gather twice a week at a local park to walk for 40 minutes. They end each walk with a devotion, prayer, and light breakfast at a nearby restaurant.

2. *Widow/widower support groups.* The Forerunners have recently started support groups for seniors whose loved ones have passed on in the last few years. Each meeting opens with prayer, and then the senior adult pastor guides the group through a conversation about walking through their particular journey of grief. It is a very sensitive time, a warm and supportive experience. "We have learned," says the senior adult pastor, "that the best caregivers to those in grief are others on the same journey."

3. *Loveline.* More than 75 church members (one-third of whom are seniors) have volunteered to call their assigned shut-ins at least twice a week. The project has fostered many intergenerational friendships and guarantees that the homebound are not isolated from the rest of the church family.

4. *Love letters.* About 35 Forerunners send encouragement cards to church members who are going through difficult times. Every month they receive a new list of names, addresses, and profiles of people who could use a lift. Letters are sent to a variety of church members, including single mothers, teenagers, college students, and ailing children. This is a powerful ministry that enables even shut-ins to remain active in the church.

5. *Sunshine company.* Six teams of two senior adults regularly assist the senior adult pastor in visiting the homebound. Each week these lay visitors are given the names, addresses, and profiles of shut-ins they are to visit. Four times a year, their dedication is acknowledged by being treated to breakfast by the church.

6. *Meals in Jesus' name.* More than 30 senior women have volunteered to take hot meals to ailing church members of all ages. A small card and a tiny bouquet accompany each meal.

7. *Forerunner-family ties.* About 200 volunteer Forerunners are paired with church families to support and pray daily for them for six months. Sponsors receive a profile and picture of their "adopted" family and are encouraged to call, write, or visit this family during the six-month period. This ministry helps bond seniors with younger members of the church and prompts them to be more understanding and aware of the tremendous pressures facing families today.

8. *Forerunner-teen friendship ties.* One year the group "adopted" about 150 teenagers in the church's youth department. Some of the friendships kindled through this ministry still exist! At the end of six months of praying for their teens, the Forerunners invited them to a banquet in which seniors were encouraged to dress like teens, and teens were to dress like grandpas and grandmas. According to the senior adult pastor, this was a huge success: "Some of the costumes were hilarious. And our teens began to see senior adults as 'real' people who cared about them and had a great sense of humor."

9. *Monthly banquets.* The monthly Forerunner banquets are not just for fun and fellowship. At each banquet they strive to break down age, income, and health barriers, not only to become better acquainted, but also to inspire nonbelievers to come to church. Both Christians and non-Christians from throughout the community are invited to attend these events, which are intended to be an entertaining and nonthreatening example of Christian life. About 25 newcomers attend each month and are later called to see if they currently go to church. If not, they are asked if they would be interested in attending. Names of prospects are given to officers of the Sunday School for further follow-up. These banquets have been the catalyst for about 40 seniors committing their lives to Jesus Christ in the last five years.

10. *Monthly trips.* Forerunners take 12 day trips a year to interesting locations. The journeys are highlighted by prayer, testimonies, and joyful singing along the way.

11. *Retreats.* Forerunners have two retreats a year, usually meeting with seniors from other churches in the denomination. They also take an extended trip in the fall to various parts of the United States.

12. *"Forerunner Forecast."* This monthly newsletter lists upcoming events and provides interesting profiles about various seniors, as well as spiritual, medical, housing, and retirement tips. It is mailed to more than 1,100 seniors in the community.

A third type of activity for this group centers on outreach and discipleship. Forerunners believe that, since Jesus put no age limit on the Great Commission, senior adults are not excused to "mark time" before He returns. Instead, they are to join younger believers in going out and making disciples. "A well-rounded senior adult ministry should accentuate the role seniors need to play in reaching others for Christ," says the senior adult pastor. Part of that responsibility involves an outreach to the approximately 70 retirement homes in the area. The Forerunner ministry is working continually toward the vast harvest of elderly people who are running out of time to enter God's kingdom. In addition, to help spread the Good News, the Forerunners have implemented or are planning the following service-oriented ministries in the local community:

1. *Convalescent-home outreach.* This year Forerunners will train 15 worship teams from the younger adult Sunday School classes to conduct worship services in convalescent homes. Each team will consist of singers, musicians, and a lay preacher. They hope to impact at least five more convalescent homes with the message of the gospel in the coming months.

2. *Christmas wish and witness.* The group is going to local retirement centers to find elderly seniors who have no family or friends. The goal is to find out what these seniors would like for Christmas, then pass the gift request, along with a picture and profile, to members of the church. This will connect the church family with older people who are lonely and hurting. Volunteers will be asked to hand-deliver the gifts and com-

mit to making three more calls on the "adopted" senior during the year.

3. *Community service.* Forerunners are encouraged to take part in community projects that help others on a personalized basis. Many are now serving by reading for the blind, delivering food and clothes to the poor in Mexico, making blankets for homeless youth. To foster more involvement in community service, the *Forerunner Forecast* has featured a "Volunteer of the Month" article, profiling the work of a serving senior.

4. *Forerunner forum.* In the next year, the senior adult leaders plan to introduce a series of Saturday seminars on important topics of interest to senior adults. These seminars will be open to the community and will include drivers' training classes (to obtain lower insurance rates). Choosing the right retirement home, health tips to live longer and better, and the latest on Medicare are some of the subjects to be covered.

Senior adults at this church learn quickly that a young, sound body is never required for acceptance by God or service to God. The idea that an older person is less worthy or less capable of serving in the church runs contrary to the fundamental message of Christian faith. Senior believers, whether able to walk or confined in a wheelchair, have Kingdom work to do, the senior adult pastor says. It is the role of a Spirit-filled senior adult ministry to promote the Kingdom work by glorifying God and witnessing His love and presence to the next generation. And is that not what Christian "spirituality" is all about?

The Forerunners have discovered many effective ways to stimulate the spiritual growth of its members—which is but one reason why this senior adult ministry is thriving. Of course, not all of the Forerunner projects may seem practical for *your* church, but at least some of them can be easily adapted to fit the needs and resources of any congregation that wants to "live in accordance with the Spirit [of God]" (Rom. 8:5).

11

Provide Recreational, Social, and Physical Activities

S eniors enjoy a good time as much as anyone else. They like to laugh, to travel, to socialize—and they want to be healthy.

Plan every meeting to include lots of laughter and joy! One senior group I know of plans at least one program quarterly devoted just to humor. This is a time when each participant comes prepared to share a humorous experience, a funny story, or a helpful anecdote. It is always a rousing success and has the largest attendance of all programs. Another senior adult group has a "good humor man" (actually a lady).

For centuries, laughter and positive emotions have been known to contribute to health, healing, and happiness. Scripture records that "a cheerful heart is good medicine, but a crushed spirit dries up the bones" (Prov. 17:22).

There is healing power in being able to laugh at oneself, at the foolishness of the world, at problems. In my own experience, while I was in physical therapy recovering from a stroke, I determined to build relationships through humor. Since doctors, nurses, and therapists hear so many complaints and negativisms, I tried beginning each therapy session by sharing a joke or humorous story. It turned out that even some of my dumbest little quips made their way around the hospital. One day, the joke I told my therapist was about the young snake who came to its mother and asked, "Mother, are we poisonous?"

"Yes," replied its mother, "very, very poisonous. Why do you ask?"

The little snake answered, "Because I just bit my tongue!"

When a different therapist asked me a few days later if I had heard about the young snake, I realized that many people had enjoyed my humor therapy.

In the book *Live Long and Love It!* there are four suggestions on how to cultivate humor.[1] We recommend that every senior adult secure a copy and practice the concepts set forth.

TRAVEL

The ancient Hohokum Indians who lived near what is now Tucson, Arizona, left their mark with a number of fascinating pictographs on a mound of rocks west of the city. Sitting on the rocks and running one's hand over the indentations made by these Indians hundreds of years ago is a thrilling experience. As I sat there tracing the primitive drawings with my fingers, I began to visualize the people who made the original designs and marvel at what they told me about the Hohokum society. This illustrates just one of the enjoyments of travel.

Why do seniors like to travel? In particular, why do most successful senior groups include travel in their activities?

1. *Travel establishes a link to other times and other cultures.* In visiting historic places, one's life is seen as part of the ongoing saga of human civilization. Others have been here before us and others will follow. This realization subconsciously provides continuity and meaning to life. Travel and study create a sense of wonder, a bonding with people we will never know.

2. *Travel provides new experiences and excitement.* Relieved from the responsibilities of child rearing and work sched-

ules, seniors have a freedom that encourages a desire to visit unfamiliar places and enjoy new experiences. Many seniors, aware that they will not live forever, are eager to travel and see what else life has to offer.

3. *Travel pampers people.* While there can be unexpected or difficult situations, in most cases travel means eating out, the luxury of being chauffeured around, the pleasure of having one's bed made and room cleaned. We all like to be pampered, and travel both fuels and satisfies that desire.

4. *Travel creates a new social environment.* Friendships blossom and new relationships are established as common experiences bring people closer together. Many older adults begin to lead cloistered lives if they no longer have a loved one with whom to travel. Group-sponsored trips provide the opportunity for both singles and couples to share adventures that would be far less rewarding and fun if experienced alone.

In making travel plans, consider trips with a purpose. The benefits from travel can be greatly heightened if the aim is not just recreation. For example, I was in Michigan when some senior adults were about to leave their church in an RV caravan of about 20 vehicles. As we waved good-bye, the laughing, excited group started for Mexico. They were on their way for the second year to work on a Christian campsite for Mexican children and youth. These seniors were combining new experiences, new sights, new culture, and new environment with fulfilling their desire to help others. Travel that is only self-serving soon wears thin, much like endless rounds of golf can become boring after a while.

A similar type of travel-with-a-purpose is encouraged by the Southern Baptists. As a denomination, they actively recruit seniors to help in building churches and in other projects that communicate the gospel outside their local area. Every denomination and local church should provide such opportunities for their senior adults.

Short excursions sponsored by local churches also provide an excellent reason to invite older adults who do not attend the church or its senior activities. Whether it be a three-day trip to enjoy fall colors or a day trip to a local point of interest, most nonaffiliated seniors would return from such a trip having had an enjoyable time and also moved closer toward being part of the group on a regular basis.

SOCIAL OUTLETS

The word *social* is a weak term for what we are trying to communicate, because we are really talking about building meaningful networks and friendships. An effective senior adult group accomplishes this by creating a *loving* atmosphere.

Allowing love to flow freely through your group will provide a ministry that has depth, height, and group breadth. It will change the group from an ordinary "social" club to a special fellowship whose members glow with enthusiasm for the program and relationships with each other.

The power of love may be mysterious, but it has never been a secret. History and literature are full of famous quotations about love. Victor Hugo wrote in *Les Misérables:* "The great happiness of life is the conviction that we are loved . . . loved for ourselves, or rather, loved in spite of ourselves." Martin Luther recognized this universal human need in his comment that "faith, like light, must always be simple and unbending; while love, like warmth, should beam forth on every side and bend to every necessity of our brethren." To this could be added William Penn's observation that "love is the hardest lesson in Christianity; but for that reason, it should be most our care to learn it."[2]

Of course, we need go no further than the New Testament to learn the importance of love. Jesus' repeated commands to love one another (e.g., Matt. 22:39; John 13:34; 15:12) are reflected in Paul's words that "if I . . . have not love, I am nothing" (1 Cor. 13:2).

Today there are many indications that love is necessary for survival. One study found that people who live alone and have few or no close friends have a mortality rate equal to that of two-pack-a-day cigarette smokers.[3] It has also been proven that people without loving support in time of sickness take longer to recover. In serious cases, patients without the caring support of friends and family die sooner than those who know their lives have value to others.

We can't make it entirely on our own. The human being has the longest dependency period of any living organism. We begin life with a love need, and we never completely outgrow it. Any group that builds a sense of caring into its warp and woof will have taken great strides toward helping its members satisfy their basic hunger for love and belonging.

Mother Teresa, following a visit to the United States, commented, "I have seen the starving in the world, but in your country I have seen an even greater hunger—and that is the hunger to be loved. No place in all my travels have I seen such loneliness as I have seen in the poverty of affluence in America."[4] In our book *Live Long and Love It!* there are seven steps to learning to love, or learning to love better.[5] These principles should be taught to every senior adult group and integrated into its social activities.

HEALTH AND FITNESS

Because one of the greatest concerns of older adults is health and wellness, an effective ministry for seniors will regularly address health-related matters in its schedule of activities.

Good health is not something over which we have complete control, but the biblical maxim about reaping what one sows can be applied to our physical condition, in that making the right choices can increase our chances of feeling well and living longer. Recognizing this fact, many alert churches have been programming for "wellness" through health walks, exercise classes, bicycle-riding clubs, and so on. Some also have a registered nurse on staff who can provide blood-pressure checks, flu shots, dietary information, and general guidance on other health issues.

According to fitness authority and researcher Dr. Lawrence

Morehouse: "Your physiological age is extremely sensitive to the amount of use you make of your body. At a calendar age of sixty, you could be functioning like a seventy-year-old owing to an inactive life-style, or you could be going like a significantly younger person because you are active."[6]

Some older adults are vital and vigorous, while others have difficulty even getting up out of their chairs and walking from place to place. For many people, the difference is simply the result of making healthy choices. Every senior adult group should have the opportunity to learn about those choices and then be encouraged to put them into action.

12
Stimulate Intellectual Development

In the book *Live Long and Love It!* we refer to Tom and Holly Hollis of Wasilla, Alaska, as examples of senior adults who are challenged to develop their intellect.[1] Holly, the oldest child of a large Dutch immigrant family, long ago dreamed of becoming a teacher. But, as was common in those days, she had to quit high school and help with the family's living expenses. Not until her own children were grown was she able to reach one of her personal goals: completing her education.

Never a quitter, Holly first enrolled in classes at the local community college and earned her two-year degree. "One of the pleasures of attending school at my age," says Holly, "is that you have lived through most of the history the class is studying. And well, if the book was wrong about the way things happened, I stood up and told them so." Holly discovered that the brain becomes lazy over the years, so it took much concentration to excel in her studies. As a pleasant surprise, Holly found that the extra mental energy she exerted carried over into other areas of her life. Never before had she felt as sharp-witted and interested in a wide variety of topics. Enjoying the sense of

131

accomplishment she experienced as a student, Holly finished her bachelor's degree and graduated with honors.

Although Holly's husband, Tom, an electronics engineer, had always hoped to continue his education, he had decided that going back to school while supporting a family was impossible. Several times, he tried to arrange for a paid study leave, but it never worked out. In retirement, Tom enjoyed watching Holly realize her educational dreams. After Holly's graduation, Tom asked her, "Well, what do you want to do now?" Her immediate answer: "Get a master's degree."

By this time Tom had spent enough nights alone or watching Holly study to decide that *his* opportunity to get more schooling had also come. So together they commuted 40 miles each way to Alaska Pacific University, often in severe weather conditions. Holly and Tom found themselves the only "senior citizen" couple attending the university. "We kept each other going," says Tom. "We found we could share our strengths with the other, and we helped each other when the going got tough. We knew we would enjoy the subject matter, but one of the unexpected pleasures was our association with professors and the more mature students we found at the graduate level."

On May 5, 1990, Tom and Holly Hollis received their master's degrees. As the dean called their names and they walked across the stage, the entire auditorium erupted in cheers and applause. It had been a long road for both of them. Holly and Tom realized lifelong goals—and if that wasn't enough, they had fun along the way.

This story could be multiplied many thousands of times over, for today's new seniors are interested in and challenged by intellectual growth. In the video *Live Long and Love It!* a psychologist, speaking about the mental ability of older adults, says, "For years it has been believed that we begin life with a limited amount of brain cells and that these cells continue to die throughout life . . . depleting our mental capacity as we age. However, recently science has discovered that brain cells, like all other body cells, continue to replace themselves at a rate that is related to demand. In other words, the more we use our minds, the healthier they become . . . regardless of age. Actually, most of the mental problems faced by healthy persons over sixty-five are not caused by age but by such things as drug interaction, lack of physical and mental exercise, and other conditions which are generally reversible."[2]

One important characteristic of effective senior groups is that they stimulate intellectual development. Here are a few simple guidelines for accomplishing this:

1. *Regularly plan activities to encourage mental growth.* Have quality speakers and educational field trips. Include games that challenge the mind, such as Scrabble, chess, and Trivial Pursuit.

2. *Provide a nutritious and well-balanced intellectual diet.* This applies whether you are studying Scripture or any other topic.

3. *Place thought-provoking material in the library, perhaps on a special shelf for seniors.* See that the material is circulated (have members share brief reports of especially interesting articles or chapters of a book). Publicize other written or taped material that might be a source of intellectual stimulation, especially if it might be suitable for discussion.

4. *Encourage members to get involved in an extension study course,* such as those offered by the New Senior Study Center (which is part of L.I.F.E. International) or by a local community college or your denomination's seminary.

5. *Do an analysis or needs assessment of topics and subjects that have the highest degree of interest for members of your group.* Then provide experiences that focus on these topics. Take as your model Oliver Wendell Holmes, former Supreme Court Justice, who at the age of 94 was asked why he had taken up the study of Greek. Holmes replied, "Why, my good sir, it is now or never!"

13
Make It Happen!

I am in Spain, leaning on a stone wall, looking out across a natural harbor that leads into the Atlantic Ocean. I am alone except for two boys fishing. Behind me rises a monolith of a monument dedicated to Christopher Columbus. On a hill overlooking the bay is the monastery in which Columbus stayed for a period of time as he prayed for help and guidance in his contemplated voyage of discovery. As I look out at that wide expanse of ocean I imagine the thoughts that must have passed through Columbus's mind as he looked at that same seascape some 500 years ago, about to launch forth into the unknown.

In recent times there has been a great deal of "Columbus bashing." However, knowing about Columbus gives me insight into how an explorer can turn dreams into reality. As you set your compass toward the "new world" of today's seniors, your ministry will have a better chance for success if you remember these three lessons:

1. *The first lesson is persistence.* Columbus, seeking to activate his bold idea, was finally given an audience with Queen

Isabella and King Ferdinand to obtain financial help and backing for the venture. The queen turned the request over to a committee. For five years that committee studied the plan before deciding it was impossible. Another year passed while a second committee pondered the proposal and then reported back to Queen Isabella that the venture would be too expensive. Finally, Queen Isabella put aside her war with the Moors long enough to personally consider what this persistent visionary was proposing. She gave her blessing to Columbus and his dream, which had first been proposed seven years earlier.

What we can learn from this is that when faced with resistance, we must use persistence. When we propose something new or ask people to change, we will always encounter pessimistic naysayers. You probably already know you will experience opposition as you endeavor to bring about change in your senior adult ministry. But persistence pays off.

2. *The second lesson is vision.* Scripture records, "Where there is no vision, the people perish" (Prov. 29:18, KJV). Often a vision will contradict accepted norms or procedures of the day. In Columbus's day, the established view of marine navigation was characterized by "flat-world thinking." People believed that anyone who sailed over the horizon would drop off into the void. Today we smile at such ignorance; but as Columbus sailed forth, he was severely testing his belief in what was possible.

My experience in working with senior adult groups has taught me the importance of vision—to see beyond what *is* to what *could be,* to venture past what *has been* to what *will be.* See with eyes of faith! First, as Columbus did, spend time in the chapel, seeking God's direction and blessing, and then set forth with enthusiasm toward new frontiers.

3. *A final lesson is influence.* Our actions today have a substantial effect on the events of the future. In Columbus's case, his findings launched 200 years of exploration. Many other pioneers would follow him, blazing new trails and making discoveries that would change the lives of people in future generations.

An "age quake" is soon to shake America and the entire world. What we do to prepare for the senior surge can change the course of future events, perhaps more than we know. The challenge now is for you to put into practice the concepts we have presented. Through your persistence, your vision, and your influence—and with God's help—the finest senior adult ministry possible can be yours. Our prayers are with you as you "go and make disciples."

Appendix
Great Growth Ideas

The following pages include "Great Growth Ideas" for your older adult ministry. They are organized into four ministry areas: (1) Spiritual Growth, (2) Service, (3) Fellowship, and (4) Evangelism. These four areas represent, in the view of the authors, the foundation blocks on which an effective older adult ministry must be built. The ideas are included to spark your imagination. Start with them, adapt them, build on them, improve them. But be sure to include at least one great growth idea (ours or yours) from each of the four areas in your coming year's activities.

Ministry Area: Spiritual Growth
Great Growth Idea 1

In His Steps

A one-week emphasis encouraging group members to ask, "What would Jesus do?" "Indeed, this is your calling. For Christ suffered for you and left you a personal example, so that you might follow in his footsteps" (1 Pet. 2:21, PHILLIPS).

How to Do It

This activity is particularly meaningful in the Lenten season, but it is a helpful spiritual growth experience anytime. On a Sunday morning, ask each member to consider focusing throughout the entire week on the question: "What would Jesus do?" And not only to ask the question but also to make an attempt to do the same thing they feel Jesus would do.

This one-week adventure is quite simple. Each morning you begin with a time of prayer and study. You focus on one specific attitude of Christ that you will emulate during that day. (See below for a suggested list and Scripture references.) Then, in the evening review your day and evaluate your experiences. It will be particularly helpful if you can share your experiences with someone close to you.

Paul said, "Be imitators of God, therefore, as dearly loved children" (Eph. 5:1).

Monday
Today's Christlike quality: Acceptance
(Read John 8:1-11.)

Jesus modeled acceptance. Everyone else saw the adulterous woman as a worthless outcast and sinner to be ostracized and put to death. But Jesus saw her differently. How did He show acceptance? He did not condone the woman's behavior, but He accepted her as a human being created in the image of God. Jesus offered her a second chance. Jesus gives people a second chance because those of us who are trying to follow Christ know we have failed and will fail in the future. But Jesus continues to love and accept us . . . and give us another chance. Visualize the Lord sitting beside you, and thank Him for accepting you, dying for you, and giving you many "second chances." Then ask Him to help you see people as He sees them, through the eyes of acceptance.

Tuesday
Today's Christlike quality: Patience
(Read 1 Cor. 13:4.)

Patience, as described in Scripture, is not the ability to spend time in a traffic jam without experiencing frustration. The word Paul uses for patience describes a person who has been wronged and has the power to avenge himself or herself but chooses not to do so.

Jesus is the perfect model of patience. Consider His attitude as He stood before His accusers prior to His crucifixion: "He was oppressed and he was afflicted, yet he never said a word. He was brought as a lamb to the slaughter, and as a sheep before her shearers is dumb, so he stood silent before the ones condemning him" (Isa. 53:7, TLB).

Most of us will never suffer as Jesus did. But as Paul said in his letter to the Romans, "We can rejoice, too, when we run into problems and trials for we know that they are good for us— they help us learn to be patient" (5:3, TLB).

One of Christ's attributes was undoubtedly patience.

Wednesday
Today's Christlike quality: Kindness
(Read John 11:1-45.)

What can we learn about Christ from this experience? What did He do in this situation? "Jesus wept" (11:35).

The dictionary defines "kindness" as "showing sympathy, concern, or understanding." Obviously, we can't raise people from the dead, but we can share in their sorrow and grief. We can share sympathy and concern for them.

To be kind to people we need to understand them. This requires careful listening. The challenge today is to really see, hear, and understand others' needs. We can imitate Jesus by walking in the shoes of others.

Remember that Jesus understands you and your needs and is sitting beside you waiting to listen. He understands just how you feel. When we ask, "What would Jesus do?" we will practice kindness and empathy for others.

Thursday
Today's Christlike quality: Forgiveness
(Read Matt. 18:21-35.)

There is no greater example of forgiveness than the words

of Jesus on the Cross as He prayed for His executioners: "Father, forgive them; for they know not what they do" (Luke 23:34, KJV).

A characteristic modeled by Jesus was to forgive those who hurt Him. "Be kind and compassionate to one another, forgiving each other, just as in Christ God forgave you" (Eph. 4:32). "Love . . . does not hold grudges and will hardly even notice when others do it wrong" (1 Cor. 13:5, TLB).

How forgiving are you?

Friday
Today's Christlike quality: Generosity
(Read 2 Cor. 9:6-15.)

"Love is . . . never haughty or selfish . . . Love does not demand its own way" (1 Cor. 13:4-5, TLB).

Think about Jesus' life, as described in the New Testament. He always put others' needs ahead of His own. Love, as demonstrated by our Lord, could easily be spelled "G-I-V-E." Throughout His earthly ministry Jesus gave and gave and gave, finally giving the ultimate gift of love—His life.

"We know what real love is from Christ's example in dying for us" (1 John 3:16, TLB).

Do you remember the Lord's words to His disciples the night before His death? "I demand that you love each other as much as I love you. And here is how to measure it—the greatest love is shown when a person lays down his life for his friends; and you are my friends if you obey me" (John 15:12-14, TLB).

Saturday
Today's Christlike quality: Well-mannered
(Read Col. 4:5-6.)

Sometimes we forget to be polite and courteous when we are at home with our families and friends. Other times we are discourteous to persons who provide a service to us (waitress, gas station attendant, grocery store clerk, etc.). After an entire week of being on our good behavior at work or school, we often are insensitive to the feelings of those we do not have to impress. But our "weekend life" is also an important place to ask, "What would Jesus do?" Family, close friends, and associates need acceptance, patience, kindness, forgiveness.

Note: A set of 50 attractive 1" x 2½" self-adhesive stickers, with the words "What Would Jesus Do?" is available from Church Growth, Inc. (1-800-844-9286) for $9.99. These can be a helpful resource to make this special spiritual growth emphasis even more meaningful.

Great Growth Idea 2

Discover Spiritual Journaling

Teach and encourage members to keep a spiritual journal for the coming month. "Then we your people, the sheep of your pasture, will praise you forever; from generation to generation we will recount your praise" (Ps. 79:13).

How to Do It

Spiritual journaling is a way for Christians to enhance their walk with God and their journey toward Christlikeness. Most people do not keep a spiritual journal but would find the experience to be an invigorating and enlightening one. Below are some comments about the process of spiritual journaling:

What is spiritual journaling? Journaling is an undiscovered source of spiritual growth. A journal is a daybook—a place to record daily happenings. But it is far more than that. A journal is also a tool for self-discovery, an aid to concentration, a mirror for the soul, a place to generate and capture ideas, a safety valve for the emotions, a training ground for the writer, and a good friend and confidant.

The benefits of spiritual journaling. Ronald Klug *(How to Keep a Spiritual Journal)* gives the following six benefits of spiritual journaling:

1. *Growth in self-understanding.* If we are to be victorious Christians, useful to God and to other people, we need to know ourselves, our temperaments, our gifts, our strengths, and our weaknesses. This is no easy process. The apostle James wrote of a man who "looks at his face in a mirror and, after looking at himself, goes away and immediately forgets what he looks like" (1:23-24). Keeping a journal can be a way to avoid that kind of forgetfulness.

2. *Guidance and decision making.* As Christians, we want our lives to conform to God's will. We know that what He wants for us is best. In some areas of our lives, we have clear guidance from God's Word. But in many specific areas of our lives, discerning God's will is more difficult. When we're faced with a decision, we can weigh the alternatives in our journal before making the decision. Then, because we have a record of the whole process, we can later recall why we decided as we did and how God used our searching to help show us the way.

3. *Making sense and order of life.* After a hectic day or week loaded with events and people and problems, many people find a great sense of peace by sitting down with their journal in the presence of God and sorting out their life; regaining perspective.

4. *Releasing emotions and gaining perspective.* A variety of feelings surge within us during a given day or week: happiness, anger, depression, joy, jealousy, fear, thankfulness. A journal can help us handle our emotions. First of all, we can diffuse emotions by expressing them in writing. Bottling up emotions, especially negative ones like anger or depression, only makes them worse. If we try to ignore them because we think "Christians shouldn't feel that way," we may be setting ourselves up for a major emotional crisis.

5. *Greater awareness of daily life.* Arthur Gordon writes: "How do we keep in the forefront of our minds the simple fact that we live in an indescribably wonderful world? It's not easy. Routine dulls the eye and the ear. Repetition and familiarity fog the capacity for astonishment. Even so, moments come to all of us when everything suddenly seems fresh and new and marvelous. Journal writing can help us nourish the 'gift of awareness.'"[1]

6. *Working through problems.* In the normal course of life we face a succession of problems—at work, at home, in our relationships, in church life. In a journal, we can "talk out" a problem, gain perspective on it, and sooner or later find a God-pleasing solution. A journal is not a substitute for people, but the journal can become a friend and confidant, especially when we have no person to talk with

What do you include in a journal?
- Personal events
- Reactions to events
- Conversations
- Prayers
- Questions
- Memories
- Insights
- Joys
- Achievements
- Failures
- World events
- Your readings
- Quotations
- Letters
- Travel
- Other materials (drawings, clippings, photos)

Some questions to get you started:

1. As I look back on the day, what were the most significant events?

2. In what ways was this day unique, different from other days?

3. Did I have any particularly significant conversations?

4. Did I do any reading? What were my reactions to it?

5. How did I feel during the day? What were the emotional high points and low points? Why did I feel as I

did? Is God trying to tell me anything through these feelings?

6. Did I find myself worrying about anything today? Can I turn that worry into a prayer?

7. What were the chief joys of the day?

8. What did I accomplish today?

9. Did I fail at anything? What can I learn from this?

10. Did I have any insights into myself or another person that I want to preserve?

Great Growth Idea 3

Goal-Setting for Personal Growth

Encourage members to set a personal growth goal for (1) Bible study, and (2) individual prayer for the coming month. "But grow in the grace and knowledge of our Lord and Savior Jesus Christ. To him be glory both now and forever!" (2 Pet. 3:18).

How to Do It

When we set personal goals, we are more likely to accomplish things than when we do not have goals. Goals in our spiritual life can help us grow in wisdom and stature with God. The purpose of this growth idea is to help members in your group discover the personal joy of setting and pursuing spiritual growth goals.

Two areas in which the spiritual life of most people can grow are *personal prayer life* and *Bible study*. If members set a personal goal in these two areas, they will find much growth to be had.

Ask each member to consider the following:

PERSONAL PRAYER LIFE. Prayer is our direct "telephone line" to God, himself. He wants to hear from us as earnestly as anyone desires a call from a loved one. And just as our human relationships grow stagnant through lack of communication, our spiritual relationship grows stale without regular communication. Perhaps the most important step in our spiritual growth journey is regular and meaningful prayer with God.

Scripture. "Be joyful in hope, patient in affliction, faithful in prayer" (Rom. 12:12).

Growth goal challenge. Consider how many times in the coming month you would like to spend time in prayer. This does not mean just the occasional utterance of a one-line prayer at work or walking down the street. It means planned, focused, uninterrupted time in prayer.

While each member is encouraged to consider his or her own life, time, and priorities, here is one way to state a prayer goal:

30 scheduled appointments with God in the next month.

BIBLE STUDY. Scripture reading, study, and application is the best means to learn what becoming Christlike means. Through careful examination, the Bible gives us a clear description of our model—Jesus Christ—and what we are called to be and do. Without Bible study, we are limited to our own short-sighted guesses of what being a Christian is all about. With a systematic study of God's Word, we can clearly see what God calls us to be and do.

Scripture. "Do your best to present yourself to God as one approved, a workman who does not need to be ashamed and who correctly handles the word of truth" (2 Tim. 2:15).

Growth goal challenge. Consider how many times in the coming month you would like to read and study a passage from the Bible.

While each member is encouraged to consider his or her own life, time, and priorities, here is one way to state a Bible study goal:

Reading and meditating on a Bible passage
30 times in the coming month.

Great Growth Idea 4

Prayer Focus

A special intercessory prayer emphasis that focuses on each person in the senior adult group. "The prayer of a righteous man has great power in its effects" (James 5:16, RSV).

How to Do It

Prayers are not always specific and directed, often because people don't know the needs of others around them. This activity will help members develop a sense of corporate concern and united prayer, as others pray for them and they pray for others.

Give every person in your group an enlarged copy of the Personal Prayer Summary Sheet (see sample below) and the assignment to complete it prior to the next meeting.

Assign one day in the next month to each person. (If there are more people than days, assign two or more people per day. If there are more days than people, assign two or more days per person.)

When you have received a copy of each person's Personal Prayer Summary Sheet, make copies (one copy for each person) and distribute a set to each person in the group. Explain that the day noted will be the day everyone in the group is to pray for that person. They should thank God for him or her and petition God for special prayer requests.

In subsequent meetings, ask persons for any feedback on their experiences.

PERSONAL PRAYER SUMMARY SHEET

Name: _____

Summarize your present living arrangement:

What things do you *wish for?*

What things do you *wonder about?*

What things do you *worry about?*

What have you recently been asking God for?

Ministry Area: Service

Great Growth Idea 1

Random Acts of Kindness

Have a two-week emphasis encouraging members to practice random acts of kindness in their daily lives. "The King will reply, 'I tell you the truth, whatever you did for one of the least of these brothers of mine, you did for me'" (Matt. 25:40).

How to Do It

This activity will help members rediscover the joy of unconditional giving and the great joy that is experienced as a result. It is simply a matter of looking for specific things to do for people in need in the name of Jesus.

In his book *Conspiracy of Kindness,* Steve Sjogren notes that demonstrating the kindness of God by offering to do some act of humble service with no strings attached has a number of benefits:

- the mere offer to serve others holds great power
- the goal in servant evangelism is to shine the spotlight on God's kingdom by coming in the spirit of Jesus
- free service offers a picture of the grace of God

Encourage each member to look for at least one thing he or she can do each day as an anonymous act of kindness. The benefit of anonymity is that it helps individuals experience the joy of helping without any expectation of return, even of a "thank you."

This unconditional nature of the kind act provides first-hand experience into the nature of unconditional giving. So often we tend to expect some sign of gratitude or appreciation from those we help. And if we don't get it, we are somewhat offended. But the spirit of God's love is one that does not require gratitude. It is purely unconditional.

Following the two-week emphasis (and perhaps in the middle of the two weeks, if your group meets then), ask for reports from members as to what they did and how they felt. Encourage members to consider adopting this approach as a lifestyle. Particularly when they may be feeling emotionally down for some reason, go out and help someone in some way. It's a great pick-me-up!

"Be careful not to do your 'acts of righteousness' before men, to be seen by them. If you do, you will have no reward from your Father in heaven" (Matt. 6:1).

Great Growth Idea 2

Life Support Mentoring

Match older adults who have experienced a life-changing event with persons who are (or will soon be) experiencing that same event. "Let the wise listen and add to their learning, and let the discerning get guidance" (Prov. 1:5).

How to Do It

Identify those senior adults who have experienced major surgery, physical challenges, or life-changing events in the past five years, and invite any who would like to, to be mentors for those who will be experiencing these same events. Here are some steps to see this significant ministry become a reality:

1. Review the Life Transition Scale below and identify any seniors who have experienced one or more of these events. (This scale was first developed by two physicians at the University of Washington Medical School as stress-producing events that commonly precipitate a coronary. The associated points indicate the relative strength/weight of each event.)

2. Have the persons in your group who have experienced one of these events meet together as a group and list the needs they felt at the time and the needs most people would have during this transition time in their life.

3. Have the group discuss and then make a specific list of how an individual or a group could respond to the needs of a person experiencing this transition event.

4. Have the group develop a curriculum for a two-hour training course for life support mentors who would be willing to be "on call" when a person encounters this particular situation. In other words, what training would help a mentor to be most effective in supporting a person during such a time of need.
5. Offer the course to anyone in the church who has had this particular life experience and is willing to be a life support mentor.
6. When someone in the church or community (church member or nonmember) experiences such an event, contact the life support mentor and ask him or her to contact the person in need.

LIFE TRANSITION SCALE

Adult Age Life Event   Rank

1. Death of a spouse	100
2. Divorce	73
3. Move to nursing/retirement home	70
4. Marital separation	65
5. Death of a close family member	64
6. Major physical problems	53
7. Marriage or remarriage	50
8. Realizing a personal lack of dreams/purpose	47
9. Financial loss of retirement money	47
10. Forced early retirement	46
11. Unable to drive	45
12. Marital reconciliation	45
13. Retirement	45
14. Spouse confined to retirement home	45
15. Change of health of family member	44
16. Gain a new family member	39

17. Change in financial state 38
18. Death of a close friend 37
19. Difficulty in getting medical insurance 36
20. Change in number of arguments with spouse 35
21. Mortgage over $100,000 31
22. Foreclosure of mortgage/loan 30
23. Sense of not being needed 29
24. Outstanding personal achievement 28
25. Spouse begins or stops work 26
26. Significantly decreased contact with children or friends 25
27. Revision of personal habits 24
28. Significantly less contact with support group(s) 24
29. Trouble with the boss 23
30. Minor physical problems 20
31. Change in recreation habits 19
32. Change in church activities 19
33. Change in social activities 18
34. Loans of less than $100,000 17
35. Change in sleeping habits 16
36. Change in number of family get-togethers 15
37. Change in eating habits 15
38. Vacation 13
39. Christmas 12
40. Minor law violation 11

Great Growth Idea 3

Helping Hands

Match older adults who have skills in household repair with persons inside or outside the church who have repair needs. "This service that you perform is not only supplying the needs of God's people but is also overflowing in many expressions of thanks to God" (2 Cor. 9:12).

How to Do It

Take an inventory of those senior adults in your group who have an interest in providing help to members and nonmembers with their household repair needs.

Next, list the various tasks that your group is able to provide. Some of the tasks may require more knowledge or experience (such as plumbing, electrical repair, mending, etc.), while other tasks may be done by most anyone (painting, gardening, vacuuming, etc.).

Third, develop an attractive flyer or brochure describing the free services available through your senior adult group and a phone number for how to contact the group. In the flyer, note that this service is available as a ministry of the senior adult group and that anyone in need qualifies. Some persons may not wish to call for themselves but may call on behalf of a neighbor, friend, or family member.

Here is a starting list of "services" that might be provided by older adults in your group:

Outside

- Gardening and weeding
- Lawn mowing and fertilizing
- Painting
- Garage repair
- Window washing
- House washing
- Car washing
- Driveway and sidewalk repair
- Pick up leaves

Inside

- Vacuuming
- Carpet cleaning
- Drapery cleaning and hanging
- Painting
- Appliance and electrical repair
- Clothes mending
- Computer installation
- Furniture repair
- House cleanup

Great Growth Idea 4

Marriage Mentoring

Match older adult couples with young engaged or newly married couples for mentoring on healthy marriages. "Listen to advice and accept instruction, and in the end you will be wise" (Prov. 19:20).

How to Do It

Ask for volunteers among any older adult couples in your group who have been married for 35+ years and would be willing to devote two nights a month to meeting with a young married/engaged couple.

The purpose of the meetings would be to develop a relationship between the two couples that would allow for sharing and growth (particularly in the younger couple) in the area of a healthy marriage.

The times together would be flexible as to the agenda but should include the discussion of a book or video on healthy Christian marriage. The meetings should be in either of the two couples' homes (although they may occasionally go out to a restaurant or some other social event).

Conversation would focus on key areas of marriage relationships and share mutual experiences and issues. The younger couple should understand that this relationship is for the purpose of learning from people who have been through many issues and survived with a marriage intact.

Topics might include:

- communication
- finances
- trust
- child-raising
- sex
- careers
- in-laws

Perspectives on Mentoring

What is "mentoring"? Definition of *mentoring*—"a relational process in which a mentor, who knows or has experienced something, transfers that something (wisdom, advice, information, experience, confidence, emotional support) to a mentoree at an appropriate time and manner so that it facilitates development and empowerment."[2]

Characteristics of successful mentors:

- *Discernment*—the ability to readily see potential in a person
- *Tolerance*—of mistakes, brashness, abrasiveness, and the like in order to see that potential develop
- *Flexibility*—in responding to people and circumstances
- *Patience*—knowing that time and experience are needed for development
- *Perspective*—having vision and ability to see down the road and suggest the next steps that a mentoree needs

Characteristics of successful mentorees:

- Desire to serve God and be used by Him
- Sense that the mentor could help them in reaching their goal
- Sense that God was involved in bringing about this mentoring relationship
- Willingness to sacrifice and give up some rights in exchange for being mentored
- A servantlike heart toward the mentor
- Willingness to accept ministry tasks given by the mentor
- Respect for the mentor
- Willingness to be held accountable by the mentor

Great Growth Idea 5

Discover Your Spiritual Gift

Help members of your senior adult group learn about, discover, and use their spiritual gift. "Now concerning spiritual gifts, brethren, I do not want you to be uninformed" (1 Cor. 12:1, KJV).

How to Do It

The New Testament speaks about spiritual gifts and how the Holy Spirit has given such gifts to every believer. Yet not many Christians, including senior adults, know much about this area. Fewer still have actually participated in a process of discovering their own spiritual gifts. And even fewer are consciously or intentionally using their gifts in ministry.

You can help your senior adults discover a whole new identity and contribute to the Body of Christ and the growth of His Church by leading a course on spiritual gifts discovery.

The course you lead for your older adults should follow the general outline below. (If you do teach a class on spiritual gifts, you are encouraged to read a book or two first on this subject.)

Spiritual Gifts—An Overview

What are "spiritual gifts"? A commonly accepted definition of a "spiritual gift" is "a special attribute given by the Holy Spirit to every member of the Body of Christ, according to God's grace, within the context of the Body."[3]

Throughout the New Testament, and particularly in three specific chapters, spiritual gifts are named. If you do some research yourself, you will find the following list of gifts from these three passages:

- From Rom. 12: prophecy, service, teaching, exhortation, giving, leadership, and mercy
- From 1 Cor. 12 (in addition to the list given in Romans): wisdom, knowledge, faith, healing, miracles, discernment, tongues, interpretation of tongues, apostle, helps, and administration
- From Eph. 4 (in addition to those already listed): evangelist, pastor

Discovering Your Spiritual Gift

How do you find out what your spiritual gifts are? And how do you help others discover their gifts? Peter Wagner believes there are several "prerequisites" that must be considered before one can begin searching for his or her spiritual gift:

1. *You must be a Christian.* God reserves the gifts of the Holy Spirit for the members of His Body, those who have a personal relationship and commitment to Jesus Christ.

2. *You must believe you are gifted.* The Bible teaches that "to each one the manifestation of the Spirit is given for the common good" (1 Cor. 12:7).

3. *You must want to discover your gift.* It means work, study, prayer, and commitment.

Most writers and authorities on the subject generally concur as to the process of discovering one's spiritual gift(s). Here are six steps that synthesize these writings:

1. *Pray.* Ask God for understanding and wisdom about spiritual gifts and for direction in discovering your own gift. Thank Him for His grace in giving you gifts, and dedicate your search for and use of your gifts to His honor. Commit yourself and your unique gifts to the growth of His Church.

2. *Study.* Read books, study the gifts passages in the Bible, know what gifts God has given to His Body and how they manifest themselves. Talk with and observe people who have the gift(s) you are exploring. Ask them how they discovered their gift and what reinforcing events contributed to their discovery.

3. *Experiment.* Look around your church and endeavor to identify areas of need. Examine your concerns, remembering that many are gifted in areas for which they have a particular concern. Then experiment.

4. *Question.* What degree of satisfaction do you feel in the areas you are experimenting with? How do you feel about it? Positive feelings usually evidence fulfillment and are a clue in discovering one's gift. Negative feelings may indicate your gifts are elsewhere.

5. *Evaluate.* Are there positive results? Spiritual gifts are task-oriented—they are given for practical use in the Body of Christ. Are your efforts producing results? These questions, when truthfully answered, give clues and direction.

6. *Verify.* Look for confirmation from the Body. Do other Christians affirm your own ideas of what your gifts are? If not, you should reevaluate your thinking.

Using Your Spiritual Gifts

Once a person has discovered his or her spiritual gifts, the fun really begins: how to *use* the gift for God in ministry.

Helping your senior adults use their spiritual gifts can begin by listing the ministry activities that presently exist in your church. Once you have identified all the roles and tasks in your church (i.e., choir, teacher, usher, worship committee, food preparation, etc.), identify which spiritual gifts would be most suited for each task. (A list of definitions of each spiritual gift will be helpful in order to do this "matching" exercise most accurately. Such a list of definitions can be found in most spiritual gift textbooks.)

Ask group members to identify the roles and tasks that relate to their particular spiritual gift and whether the roles available have any appeal to them. A person with the gift of teaching, for example, should consider whether he or she would feel comfortable trying a role related to that gift.

Not all people with the gift of teaching, however, will be a good teacher. Nor will all senior adults with the spiritual gift of teaching want to volunteer to be the next junior high boys' Sunday School teacher. But hopefully there are opportunities where the gift can be used.

If there does not appear to be a specific role or task in the church that complements the older adult's spiritual gift (as well as his or her interest), consider what activities could be created that would build on this spiritual gift.

Ministry Area: Fellowship

Great Growth Idea 1

Start New Groups

Begin three to five new small groups in your senior adult ministry that reflect the interests and/or concerns of group members. "The intelligent man is always open to new ideas. In fact, he looks for them" (Prov. 18:15, TLB).

How to Do It

One of the best ways for a senior adult (church member or nonmember) to build meaningful relationships that will strengthen his or her spiritual and emotional life is through involvement in a small group. Small groups provide a place for a person to give and to receive, to know and be known, to love and be loved.

Your older adult group can and should have a variety of smaller groups within the larger group. A good rule of thumb is 1 group for every 15 members. There are many different kinds of groups, which is good since not all older adults will prefer the same kind of group. Here is a list of just a few kinds of groups:

- Bible study group
- prayer group
- fellowship group
- social group
- task group
- accountability group
- covenant group
- house church

There are guidelines that have been tested and can be helpful in successfully starting a new group. They are listed below in the form of a question. As you are able to ask, and then answer, these questions, you will find that your new small groups will grow healthy and last long.

1. Who is our target audience?
2. What kind of group would best meet their needs?
3. How will the prospective members be identified?

4. What are the specific goals of the group, and when will they be accomplished?

5. Who will lead the group?

6. Will training be necessary for the leader? If so, how will it occur?

7. How will we promote the group and attract visitors?

8. When and where will the group meet?

9. What support will the group leader need to assure success?

10. Will this group contribute to the purpose of the church?

Great Growth Idea 2

Take a Weekend Retreat

There's nothing like spending a weekend together to get better acquainted! Seniors (members and nonmembers alike) will find an interesting weekend getaway to be a great boon to camaraderie. "But if we walk in the light, as he is in the light, we have fellowship with one another" (1 John 1:7).

How to Do It

Begin by asking members what experiences they have had in the area with good getaway places. You'll find a wealth of suggestions, and often volunteers to help coordinate a trip.

As you consider such an activity, keep two things in mind that will make for a successful weekend: (1) program, (2) people.

Program. A good balance is important. The retreat should be a blend of new experiences, good interaction, stimulating ideas, encouraging personal times and building new friendships. These will not happen without good planning of a good program.

Consider inviting a guest speaker who is commissioned to bring several helpful messages. Plan some small-group interaction and sharing time with preplanned questions and topics. Have fun, with some skits or a talent show.

People. There is no better place or way to grow a senior adult group than through a weekend retreat. So don't let it be just an "insider's" activity. Strongly encourage each older adult to personally invite a person or couple from outside the church. Your retreat will not be a success if it is only for those who are regular attenders.

Print up a flyer on the trip and give five copies to each group member, with instructions to give them to people they think would enjoy the trip. You will find that seeds are planted that will blossom at some time in the future in the form of new believers reached for Christ and the Church.

Great Growth Idea 3

Adopt a Grandchild

Develop a program of "matchmaking" between older adults in your church and young children who are looking for a grandparent. "Whoever welcomes this little child in my name welcomes me" (Luke 9:48).

How to Do It

There are many of your older adults whose grandchildren are hundreds or thousands of miles away. At the same time, there are also many children in your church who may seldom or never see their grandparents. What an opportunity!

Survey your church family to find out how many children are living more than 500 miles away from any grandparent or whose grandparents are deceased.

Next, survey your senior adults to find out how many of them would be willing to "adopt" one of these young people (or families) for the next year. This would simply mean spending a few hours at least once a month (more is certainly possible) with these children, having a special time together.

Come up with a name for your program, and write up a description of what it means to be involved. Circulate this flyer among the church family and include a contact person and phone number for parents to call.

Put a little booklet together called "What 'Grandparenting' Means." This would be given to each senior who wants to be a part of this program. The contents should describe expectations of the "Grandparent." The following list could be an outline:

What it means to be a grandparent. In the book *The Joy of Grandparenting,* Clarice Orr writes about the various mentoring, modeling, and encouraging roles that grandparents play in the lives of their grandchildren. These roles need not be limited to biological grandparents, but can apply to any "grandparent" that is a part of a child's life.

- *Grandparents are magicians*—We take out our teeth, unplug our ears, and make magic from the ordinary.

- *Grandparents are cheerleaders*—Watching, encouraging, attending, praising, inspiring, motivating, and telling our grandkids we have faith in them and will always love them.

- *Grandparents are playmates*—Being a kid again is our favorite occupation: "Grandmas are just antique little girls."

- *Grandparents are kinkeepers*—We share our heritage to provide the roots that add stability to our young families.

- *Grandparents are bridge builders*—We bridge the gaps through communication and understanding.

- *Grandparents are heroes*—We have an awesome duty to model for our youth how to live and die.

- *Grandparents are beacons*—As spiritual guides or "lighthouses," our best is just being there and praying for them.

- *Grandparents are security blankets*—We can be a safe place that provides comfort—where grandchildren will always be accepted.

- *Grandparents are sages*—With experience and knowledge, wise elders extend their skills beyond the family circle.

A large group orientation should be held twice a year with new "grandparents" and parents of prospective "grandchildren." At the meeting the grandparenting program is introduced, along with the purpose and goals. Parents should leave the meeting feeling comfortable about the program.

The first several times the "grandparents" come over to the adopted family, the whole family should be involved. Plan something fun, maybe go out to the local ice cream parlor. As the parents and children grow comfortable with the "grandparents," other events might be planned without the parents.

Here is a list of just a few things to do with "grandparents" and "grandchildren":

- go to the zoo
- visit a kids' museum
- go to the mall
- play bingo
- do a craft project

- go out for ice cream
- visit a fire station
- watch a video
- make popcorn
- read a book

Great Growth Idea 4

Special-Interest Groups

Start two or three new groups for senior adults who share something in common to get together and enjoy the company of others like them. These special interest groups should be open to members and nonmembers alike. "We loved you so much that we were delighted to share with you not only the gospel of God but our lives as well, because you had become so dear to us" (1 Thess. 2:8).

How to Do It

Conduct a survey of persons in your older adult ministry (enlarge it to the entire church if you would like). Ask them to list one or more items under each of the following topics:

- How I enjoy spending leisure time
- Issues for which I have a special concern
- Topics I would like to learn more about

Once you have tabulated the results, look for areas in which there are a large number of similar responses. Write each area down on a separate sheet of paper and attach each to a separate clipboard. At your next several meetings put the clipboards on a table in the back and ask group members to sign their names on one of the sheets if they would be interested in meeting to explore the possibility of starting a special-interest group on that topic.

Be sure to communicate that their signature is not a commitment to lead such a group, or even to participate in one. It is simply an agreement to get together with others with similar interests and talk about whether there is a desire to organize a special-interest group around that topic.

Possible kinds of special-interest groups might include:

- *a reading club* where group members select and read a book, then meet regularly to discuss it
- *a hiking club* where members explore different parks or trails in the area, perhaps taking a lunch
- *a Bible study group* where members meet to study and discuss different passages of Scripture
- *a quilting group* where members meet to share patterns and designs and work on individual or group projects
- *a widow support group* where members who have lost a spouse meet to encourage and support one another
- *a singing group* where members meet to sing the "good old songs" (secular and religious) around a piano
- *a performing group* where members who share a common interest and ability (singing, musical instruments, drama, etc.) meet to rehearse and present their skills in public
- *a service group* where members meet together to help persons in the church or community who are in need, using their skills and knowledge

Great Growth Idea 5

Advanced Learning Classes

Ask different members of your senior adult group to consider teaching one, or a series, of classes on a topic of their particular interest. "Share with God's people who are in need. Practice hospitality" (Rom. 12:13).

How to Do It

Conduct a survey of persons in your older adult ministry concerning their particular hobbies and interests. People, older adults in particular, often have many different and fascinating areas of interest and expertise. Ask them if they would be willing to teach a class on this topic to others in the group. Be sure to invite nonmember friends to these classes; it's a great opportunity to build relationships between Christians and non-Christians.

The class could be a simple one-hour introduction, or a more extended multiple week study. It might be on a particular topic (such as gardening, woodcarving, chess, needlepoint, computers) or some kind of field trip to an area of interest/expertise (such as the zoo, an aquarium, a homeless shelter, a childcare center, symphony).

Work with the person to help him or her prepare for the class, develop handouts, copy articles, design overhead transparencies, and so forth. This time of teaching will be enjoyable for those who are presenting, and intellectually stimulating for those who are learning.

Ministry Area: Evangelism

Great Growth Idea 1

Focused Prayer

Spend time as a group praying specifically for members' unreached friends and relatives. "The prayer of a righteous person has great power in its effects" (James 5:16, RSV).

How to Do It

Ask each senior adult to complete a copy of the Personal Profile below on a person in their circle of influence who is not a believer or an active member in a local church.

Divide your group into smaller groups of four people. Ask one person to share something about the friend or relative about whom they completed the Personal Profile form. Explain any additional background concerning the relationship, and share any special prayer requests. Others in the group may want to take notes on prayer requests.

The smaller group should then spend time praying specifically for this person and the relationship between the older adult and his or her friend/relative.

After each person in the group has prayed for the person, have the next person in the group share the Personal Profile about his or her friend/relative. Repeat this process until all four persons have shared and been prayed for.

Personal Profile

General Information
> Relationship and length:
> Approximate age:
> Birthday:
> Occupation:

Family
> Marital status:

Spouse's name and relevant information:

Children (names/ages):

Other Christian family/relatives:

Religious

Childhood/youth experiences (SS, camp, etc.):

Church membership (if dropout, when, why?):

Parents' attitudes toward religion:

Denominational background:

Attitude toward Christianity/our church:

Knowledge of the Bible:

Misconceptions regarding Christianity:

Other Christians he or she knows well:

Why he or she is not a Christian:

Special Interests

Hobbies:

Talents/skills:

Other interests:

Special Needs/Problems/Concerns

Other Pertinent Information

Great Growth Idea 2

Visit Another Church

Send several senior adults to visit another church in the area and report what it was like being a newcomer in that environment. "If then I do not grasp the meaning of what someone is saying, I am a foreigner to the speaker, and he is a foreigner to me" (1 Cor. 14:11).

How to Do It

Ask for volunteers from your group to visit another church in your area during the coming month. The church they select should be a church where they have no friends or relatives and have never visited before. Members should go either as a couple or singles (not as a group).

Have them complete the continuums below (placing a check on one of the seven numbers for each item), based on their visit. After they have visited the church, ask them to report to the group what their experience was. Then lead a discussion with the group on the topic of what the seniors can do to improve their own church's welcome to newcomers who are visiting for the first time.

Facility

Ease in Finding Location

1	2	3	4	5	6	7

Poor   Acceptable   Excellent

Additional comments:

First Impressions of Outside

1	2	3	4	5	6	7

Poor   Acceptable   Excellent

Additional comments:

First Impressions of Inside (upon immediately entering)

1	2	3	4	5	6	7

Poor   Acceptable   Excellent

Additional comments:

Impressions of Inside (after the service)

1	2	3	4	5	6	7

Poor   Acceptable   Excellent

Additional comments:

Parking
Adequacy of Spaces

1	2	3	4	5	6	7

Poor   Acceptable   Excellent

Additional comments:

Proximity to Entrance

1	2	3	4	5	6	7

Poor   Acceptable   Excellent

Additional comments:

Nursery
First Impressions upon Entering

1	2	3	4	5	6	7

Poor   Acceptable   Excellent

Additional comments:

Confidence in Nursery Staff and Operations

1	2	3	4	5	6	7

Poor   Acceptable   Excellent

Additional comments:

Impressions upon Leaving Nursery

1	2	3	4	5	6	7

Poor   Acceptable   Excellent

Additional comments:

Signs
Directions from Parking Area to Appropriate Building Entrance

1	2	3	4	5	6	7

Poor   Acceptable   Excellent

Additional comments:

Where to Get General Information

1	2	3	4	5	6	7

Poor   Acceptable   Excellent

Additional comments:

Directions to Sanctuary/Worship Center

1	2	3	4	5	6	7

Poor   Acceptable   Excellent

Additional comments:

Directions to Rest Rooms

1	2	3	4	5	6	7

Poor   Acceptable   Excellent

Additional comments:

Directions to Nursery

1	2	3	4	5	6	7

Poor   Acceptable   Excellent

Additional comments:

What other information/directions did you desire?

Sanctuary

First Impressions upon Entering Sanctuary/Worship Center

1	2	3	4	5	6	7

Poor   Acceptable   Excellent

Additional comments:

Visibility

1	2	3	4	5	6	7

Poor   Acceptable   Excellent

Additional comments:

Sound/Acoustics

1	2	3	4	5	6	7

Poor   Acceptable   Excellent

Additional comments:

Ease in Being Seated

1	2	3	4	5	6	7

Poor   Acceptable   Excellent

Additional comments:

Rest Rooms

First Impressions upon Entering

1	2	3	4	5	6	7

Poor   Acceptable   Excellent

Additional comments:

Education Classrooms

First Impressions upon Entering

1	2	3	4	5	6	7

Poor   Acceptable   Excellent

Additional comments:

Worship Service

Music

1	2	3	4	5	6	7

Poor   Acceptable   Excellent

Additional comments:

Welcome to Visitors

1	2	3	4	5	6	7

Poor   Acceptable   Excellent

Additional comments:

Theme

1	2	3	4	5	6	7

No clear theme   Theme seen in all activities and
                                  relevant to participants

Additional comments:

Bulletin/Program

1	2	3	4	5	6	7

Like the classified ads   Attractive, well-prepared

Additional comments:

Announcements

1	2	3	4	5	6	7

A distraction   Blends into service

Additional comments:

Response

1	2	3	4	5	6	7

No opportunity to respond   Clear response appropriate
to the message   to the message

Additional comments:

Flow

1	2	3	4	5	6	7

Various components   Each part is part of the whole
are disjointed   and fits together

Additional comments:

Language

1	2	3	4	5	6	7

Archaic with mostly   Clear communication
religious jargon   widely understood

Additional comments:

Great Growth Idea 3

Conduct an Entry Event

Plan one or more special events that will attract unchurched older adults from the community. "I brought them into the house of the LORD" (Jer. 35:4).

How to Do It

Many unchurched older adults will not attend a church, Sunday School class, or small group. An entry event can be just the thing to establish a contact and begin building a relationship with unchurched older adults.

An entry event is a high-visibility (usually one-time) activity/event sponsored by the church or senior adult group and designed to be of interest to churched and unchurched seniors in the community. The content of a good entry event will be appealing to older adults regardless of whether or not they are actively involved in church.

The assumption behind an entry event is that people change their behavior when the benefit is perceived to be greater than the cost. Therefore, their attendance at your entry event will be based on their assessment of its value vs. its cost. The goal of an effective entry event is to see a large number of unchurched adults and families attend.

Here are eight characteristics of a good entry event:

1. A variety of members are involved in defining, planning, and conducting the event.

2. Nonmembers (your target group) are also involved in defining, planning, and conducting the event.

3. The event is well-publicized.

4. The event is conducted in a neutral location.

5. The event addresses a felt interest or need that cannot be met elsewhere.

6. The event requires low risk or obligation for prospective attendees.

7. The church's purpose and appropriate opportunities for further involvement are communicated.

8. The names and addresses of participants are obtained.

Here are some sample entry events:

Holidays/Seasonal
- Valentine's Day grandfather-granddaughter and grand-mother-grandson banquet
- Christmas dinner
- Halloween/harvest festival
- 4th of July celebration
- Memorial Day picnic and parade

Family Issues
- "Effective Grandparenting" workshop
- Guest speaker on relevant topic(s)
- "Helping Your Child Through a Divorce" seminar
- "Disciplining Your Grandchild" seminar

Marital Issues
- "Marriage Tips for People 55 Years And Older" seminar
- "Preparing for the Loss of a Spouse" seminar
- Guest speaker on relevant topic(s)

Special Interests
- Visit to local points of interest
- Community picnic
- "Welcome to the neighborhood" orientation for new neighbors

- Tax planning for senior adults
- Grandparent/grandchild hike or picnic

Kids Events
- Taffy pull
- Ice cream social
- Pet show and races
- Swimming party
- Pinewood derby race

Great Growth Idea 4

Create Entry Paths

Begin several groups that would be of interest to nonmembers. "But grow in the grace and knowledge of our Lord and Savior Jesus Christ. To him be glory both now and forever!" (2 Pet. 3:18).

How to Do It

If your senior adult group decides to conduct one or more entry events (see previous growth idea), the next question is, What do you do with the names of the prospective new members you have identified through these events? The answer is to begin a series of entry paths.

An entry path is a church-sponsored program, group, or activity in which a nonmember can become involved on a regular basis. It is an ongoing function in which the nonmember can develop a longer-term relationship with people in the church.

The goal of an effective entry path is to provide an opportunity for your members to develop friendships and relationships with unchurched senior adults.

Here are seven characteristics of a good entry path:

1. The group/activity is of interest to members and non-members alike.

2. There is low risk and commitment required.

3. It is held in a neutral meeting place.

4. Prospects are personally invited.

5. Time is spent building and nurturing relationships in the group.

6. The group is composed of people who share things in common.

7. The benefit is perceived to be greater than the cost.

Here are some sample entry paths:

Sports/Physical Fitness

- Sports and recreation teams (bowling, shuffleboard, lawn bowling, checkers, etc.)
- Aerobics class or exercise group
- Weigh-down (weight loss) class
- Codependency group

Marital Issues

- Marriage enrichment class
- Couples small group
- Widow(er) recovery support group

Grandparenting Issues

- Grandparenting study/support group (book/video study)
- When grandparents raise grandchildren
- What to do when your child gets a divorce

Special Interests

- Spiritual discovery/study group
- Crafts (basket weaving, quilting, etc.)
- What does the Bible say about . . .
- Community service task force

Notes

~ ~ ~

Introduction

1. William Shakespeare, *Julius Caesar* IV, iii, 217.

2. Research Notes, "The Aging Mainlines," *Net Results,* September 1992, 11.

Chapter 1: The Church of Tomorrow

1. *Time,* January 14, 1991.

2. See "Catch the Age Wave," by Michael Maren, *Success,* October 1991, 54.

3. The purpose of this book is not to present a detailed analysis of the significant trends in our society. For more detailed discussion, see books such as *Megatrends* by John Naisbitt and *What Americans Believe* by George Barna.

4. Jill M. Richardson, "Now, That's Retirement!" *Alive,* April 1991, 4.

5. A "focus group" is a group of 10 to 12 people, gathered to discuss and clarify or focus on certain interests or concerns.

6. Elizabeth Vierck, *Fact Book on Aging* (Santa Barbara, Calif.: ABC-CLIO, 1990), 73.

7. Ibid., 72.

8. Ken Dychtwald and Joe Fowler, *Age Wave* (Los Angeles: Tarcher, 1989), 209.

Chapter 2: The Senior Surge

1. Vierck, *Fact Book on Aging,* 4.

2. Ibid., xiii.

3. Ibid., 7.

4. William M. Clements, ed., *Religion, Aging, and Health: A Global Perspective* (London: Hawthorne Press, 1989), 146.

5. Dychtwald and Fowler, *Age Wave.*

6. Vierck, *Fact Book on Aging,* 15.

7. "Sixty-Something: Part 1," *U.S. News and World Report,* April 16, 1990, 64.

8. Barbara Pittard Payne, "The Aging Spirit," *Aging Today* 12, No. 1 (February/March 1991): 14.

9. Rhea Joyce Rubin, "Aging Population Boom in Fiction," *Aging Today* 12, No. 1 (February/March 1991): 14.

Chapter 3: Developing a Christian View of Life and Aging

1. Christopher Lasch, *The Culture of Narcissism* (New York: W. W. Norton, 1979), 356.

2. *Live Long and Love It!* video (Monrovia, Calif.: Church Growth, 1990).

3. Ibid.

4. Ibid.

5. Pierre Teilhard de Chardin, *The Phenomenon of Man* (London: Collins Fontana, 1959), 256.

6. Vaclav Havel, "Points to Ponder," *Reader's Digest,* February 1991, 179.

Chapter 4: Ageism—Is It Real in the Church?

1. Lasch, *Culture of Narcissism,* 355-56.

Chapter 5: New Beginnings for Your Senior Adult Group

1. Kenneth Van Wyk, "Educate for Church Growth," *Church Growth: America,* March/April 1978, 9.

Chapter 6: Target-Group Evangelism

1. Flavil R. Yeakley, "Persuasion in Religious Influence" (doctoral dissertation, University of Illinois, 1975).

2. Fred Smith, "The Gift of Greeting," *Christianity Today* 29, 18:70.

3. Charles Arn, *Growing in Love* (Monrovia, Calif.: Church Growth, 1988).

4. *Live Long and Love It!* video.

5. Mark Bergmann, *Engaging the Aging in Ministry* (St. Louis: Concordia, 1981), 33.

6. Arnell Motz, *Reclaiming a Nation* (Winnipeg: Trinity Western Press, 1990), 163.

7. Available from most religious film libraries or from *L.I.F.E. International.*

Chapter 7: Practice *Oikos* Evangelism

1. Michael Green, *Evangelism in the Early Church* (Grand Rapids: Eerdmans, 1970), 210.

2. Charles Arn, *Growth: A New Vision for the Sunday School* (Monrovia, Calif.: Church Growth Press, 1980), 81.

Chapter 8: Incorporate Newcomers

1. Carol Spargo Pierskalla, *Rehearsal for Retirement* (Valley Forge, Pa.: National Ministries, American Baptist Churches, U.S.A., 1992), 83-85.

2. Warren J. Hartman, *A Study of the Church School in the United Methodist Church* (Nashville: Board of Education, 1972), 54.

3. E. S. Anderson, *The Sunday School Growth Spiral* (Nashville: Convention Press, 1979), 47.

4. C. Peter Wagner, lecture presented at LAMP Seminar, Pasadena, Calif.

Chapter 9: Establish a Small-Group Network

1. *The Win Arn Growth Report No. 17* (Monrovia, Calif.: Church Growth, Inc.), 3.

2. An excellent resource in the area of small-group development is *How to Start and Grow Small Groups* by Jeanne Hipp. This, plus other small-group training and curriculum material, is available from Church Growth, Inc. A free catalog is available by calling their toll-free number (1-800-423-4844).

Chapter 10: Stimulate Spiritual Growth

1. Kathleen Fischer, *Winter Grace* (New York: Paulist Press, 1985), 1.

Chapter 11: Provide Recreational, Social, and Physical Activities

1. Win and Charles Arn, *Live Long and Love It!* (Wheaton, Ill.: Tyndale House, 1991), 121.

2. Hugo, Luther, and Penn are quoted in Win Arn and Charles Arn, *Who Cares About Love?* (Monrovia, Calif.: Church Growth Press, 1986), 170, 185, 41.

3. Sheila Sobel Maramarco, "Friendship: The Tie That Binds You in Good Health," *PSA Magazine,* January 1983, 32-34.

4. Arn and Arn, *Live Long and Love It!* 139.

5. Ibid., 141.

6. Albert Myers and Christopher P. Anderson, *Success over Sixty* (New York: Summit Books, 1984), 219.

Chapter 12: Stimulate Intellectual Development

1. Arn and Arn, *Live Long and Love It!* 159-61.

2. *Live Long and Love It!* video.

Appendix: Great Growth Ideas

1. Arthur Gordon, *A Touch of Wonder* (Old Tappan, N.J.: Revell, 1974), 165.

2. Paul Stanley, *Connecting: The Mentoring Relationships You Need to Succeed in Life* (Colorado Springs: NavPress, 1992), 40.

3. Peter Wagner, *Your Spiritual Gifts Can Help Your Church Grow* (Ventura, Calif.: Regal Books, 1979), 42.